THE THIRD BOOK

OF

HORACE'S *ODES*

EDITED WITH TRANSLATION
AND RUNNING COMMENTARY

BY

GORDON WILLIAMS

OXFORD
AT THE CLARENDON PRESS
1969

Oxford University Press, Ely House, London W. 1

GLASGOW NEW YORK TORONTO MELBOURNE WELLINGTON
CAPE TOWN SALISBURY IBADAN NAIROBI LUSAKA ADDIS ABABA
BOMBAY CALCUTTA MADRAS KARACHI LAHORE DACCA
KUALA LUMPUR SINGAPORE HONG KONG TOKYO

PRINTED IN GREAT BRITAIN

PREFACE

THIS edition is designed primarily for sixth-formers and under-
graduates. It is inspired by the experience of lecturing to the General
Humanity class in St. Andrews, a responsive audience to whom I
am greatly indebted. I have found that the traditional type of com-
mentary, in which a series of difficulties are picked out separately
for comment, seriously inhibits readers from grasping the meaning
of a poem as a whole and even from understanding that poetry
(ancient no less than modern) is a form of discourse fundamentally
different from prose. Hence I have explained each poem in the
form of a continuous running commentary, which has the purpose
of subordinating the explanation of single difficulties to the ex-
position of the poet's process of thought. This is preceded by a
literal translation. The intention here is not only to help those whose
knowledge of Latin is uncertain (though it will do that well enough)
but also to provide the briefest possible explanation of the poet's
actual words. The *Introduction* is designed to be strictly functional
and provides essential information on the history of the times
(Horace's *Odes* were highly topical), the nature of poetry in Rome,
and a series of critical concepts which should be useful to the reader
in trying to appreciate Horace's poetry. Some knowledge of Greek
poetry is essential, and a series of relevant extracts are collected
(and translated) in an Appendix.

Nothing systematic is said of the textual history of *Odes*. I have
omitted discussion of this both for reasons of space (it is extremely
complex) and because little help is to be gained from a knowledge
of the textual tradition, interesting though it is in itself, in solving the
major difficulties of text in *Odes* iii. Only those questions about the
text are discussed which involve significant points of interpretation
and affect the understanding of a poem. As far as possible I have
placed such discussions in footnotes or in longer notes appended
to the running commentary.

It is true that the better a reader's knowledge of the Latin language, the better will be his understanding of Horace's *Odes*. Nevertheless, various degrees of appreciation are possible, and I have some hope that readers who are interested in poetry, outside the process of acquiring formal education, may be tempted to read the work of a poet who has earned an important place in the history of European poetry.

This is an experimental edition, and I should welcome criticisms or suggestions from readers.

My grateful thanks are due to friends and colleagues for their help: Professor C. J. Fordyce sharpened my understanding of some major problems by discussing them with me; Mr. P. A. George read an early draft and suggested a number of improvements; Dr. G. E. Rickman gave me his advice on historical problems; Mr. J. H. Simon helped me with his critical comments and meticulous proof-reading.

GORDON WILLIAMS

St. Andrews
December 1968

CONTENTS

The cover illustration is the figure of *Terra Mater* from the Ara Pacis in Rome and is reproduced with the permission of Mansell Alinari.

INTRODUCTION

I. LIFE AND WORKS

QUINTUS HORATIUS FLACCUS was born at Venusia in Apu
on 8 December 65 B.C.: he died on 27 November 8 B.C., wit
a few days of his fifty-seventh birthday. His father's family wa
servile origin, and he calls his father a freedman (*Sat.* i. 6. 6,
libertino patre natum); his father's profession was lucrative—he
an auctioneer—and he had a small holding. There was eno
money for his father to take Horace to school in Rome to fu
better education (under Orbilius) than could be got locally. He
then went on to university at Athens; he was there when Br
came, hot from the assassination of Julius Caesar, with heady
of 'Liberty', and was persuaded to serve with him as *tribunus*
tum (far too high a rank for a new recruit—something like lieute
colonel—and, also, normally reserved for men of the best fami
He participated in the disastrous defeat at Philippi in 42 B.C., esc
and returned to Rome to find all his father's property gone
confiscations. He obtained a pardon for his political 'error
purchased the post (something of a sinecure) of *scriba quae:*
keeper of the quaestors' records. He says that poverty drove l
write verse; this caught the eye of Maecenas to whom h
introduced by Virgil. So he became one of the circle of great F
writers who were collected, under the patronage of Ma
around Octavian (later Augustus). The Sabine farm was a
benefit of that patronage. But Horace remained indeper
he refused a request by Augustus to become his secretar

---

[1] In normal practice some military tribunes were elected by the people
appointed by the general (who used the opportunity to exercise patronage
of friends). Horace belonged to the latter category, and, while such tribu
have an easy time in peace, they were naturally required for real military
emergencies (as in 42 B.C.). Horace (*Satires* i. 6. 47–8) recalls how men sne
he received this appointment so far above his station. On the condition
tribunes, see R. E. Smith, *Service in the Post-Marian Roman Army*, Manche
Press, 1958, 59–62.

established a free and easy relationship (as fragments of letters show) not only with Maecenas but also with Augustus. He wrote the *Epodes* and two books of *Satires* in the decade 40–30 B.C., *Odes* i–iii between 30 and 23 B.C., *Epistles* i in 23–20 B.C., *Epistles* ii in 19–15 B.C., and *Odes* iv, following the *carmen saeculare* of 17 B.C., in 17–13 B.C. (the *Ars Poetica* cannot be dated with certainty). By 17 B.C., when the official request to write the *carmen saeculare* came, Horace had effectively become 'poet laureate' in Rome (Virgil had died in 19 B.C.) and was then addressing his poetry directly to Augustus (as he had never done before). It was a life highly productive in great poetry, but two complex factors need to be grasped if that poetry is to be properly appreciated: the political situation in the period from about 42 B.C.; and the place of the poet in Roman society and the nature of Maecenas' patronage.

2. THE POLITICAL SITUATION 42–23 B.C.

This is at once one of the most significant and also one of the most complex periods in recorded history. Only the bare bones can be suggested here; for this there is no better starting-point than the analysis by Tacitus at the beginning of his *Annals* (i. 2):

Postquam Bruto et Cassio caesis nulla iam publica arma, Pompeius apud Siciliam oppressus exutoque Lepido, interfecto Antonio ne Iulianis quidem partibus nisi Caesar dux reliquus, posito triumviri nomine consulem se ferens et ad tuendam plebem tribunicio iure contentum, ubi militem donis, populum annona, cunctos dulcedine otii pellexit, insurgere paulatim, munia senatus magistratuum legum in se trahere, nullo adversante, cum ferocissimi per acies aut proscriptione cecidissent, ceteri nobilium, quanto quis servitio promptior, opibus et honoribus extollerentur ac novis ex rebus aucti tuta et praesentia quam vetera et periculosa mallent. neque provinciae illum rerum statum abnuebant, suspecto senatus populique imperio ob certamina potentium et avaritiam magistratuum, invalido legum auxilio quae vi ambitu postremo pecunia turbabantur.

'When, after Brutus and Cassius were killed (42 B.C.), no armies were under the control of the state and Pompeius had been crushed off Sicily (36 B.C.), then, with Lepidus stripped of power (36 B.C.) and Antony killed (31 B.C.) and even the Julian party having no other leader left, Caesar, putting aside the name of triumvir and presenting himself as a consul and

content with a tribune's power for protecting the people, once he had charmed the soldiery with donatives, the people with cheap corn, all men with the delights of peace, little by little elevated himself and drew to himself the functions of senate, magistrates, and laws, with no opposition at all since the most outspoken had fallen in battle or through proscriptions, and the remainder of the *nobiles*, each in proportion to his servility, were themselves being elevated by wealth and promotion and so, profiteers of revolution, preferred safety and the present to the past and danger. The provinces also acquiesced in the new regime, since control by senate and people was suspect because of the ambitions of the great and the greed of magistrates, and the laws were powerless to help since they too were at the mercy of violence, intrigue and—in the last resort—bribery.'

This translation has deliberately preserved the inelegantly long opening sentence, for in it Tacitus has, as it were, enacted the extreme complexity of the period which he so pithily summarizes. Despair, love of epigram, and malice have pointed Tacitus' remarks, but basically it would be hard to quarrel seriously with his survey. He has committed one error which is human and understandable and is committed by most men at all times, but which must be realized by any serious reader of Horace: he has failed to distinguish between his moral judgement on the way in which Augustus gained power for himself and his political judgement on what the situation of Rome at the time demanded. Augustus gained power by a ruthless determination that spared neither friend nor enemy, and he held it by the same means for an astonishing forty-five years; he deliberately created a situation, as Tacitus says, in which he was the only surviving leader. Yet, not only is it difficult for us to think that any other political solution was open to Rome, but—more important —it must have been even more difficult for the majority of contemporaries. Here Tacitus' failure to distinguish between his moral indignation and his political judgement leads him to sneer at Augustus' enticements (*pellexit*) to the people and at the servility of the old nobility. But everyone had good reason for acquiescence.

What happened to Rome in the period after the Gracchi was a social and political revolution. Previously power had been in the hands of a small oligarchy which kept all the major offices of state within its own ranks (*nobilis* meant someone in whose family there had been the holder of the consulship) and succeeded in totally absorbing any outsider (*novus homo*) who managed to break in. But many factors, especially the need for important and lengthy campaigns at a distance from Rome, put great power into the hands of individuals who were thereby encouraged to make a bid for supreme control.[1] Yet, where one had tried, others could also, and so the half-century before 31 B.C. is filled with a series of disastrous civil wars in which a succession of aspirants tried to gain control of the state. The most successful was Julius Caesar, and after his assassins were defeated at Philippi in 42 B.C., Tacitus says that all the armies were under the control of individuals (*nulla iam publica arma*): the army of Brutus and Cassius was the last army of the Roman Republic.

This was the army in which Horace had served and it fought in vain for 'Liberty'. But men define Liberty according to their circumstances: the Liberty which perished at Philippi could be viewed as the privilege of the oligarchy, and, in the end, the liberty to conduct civil war for personal advantage. By his total success in exercising that liberty in his own interest, Augustus destroyed it and was able to present himself to the Roman people as the guarantor of peace. The majority of the people accepted him on those terms and his opponents were mainly members of the old oligarchy who regretted past privileges; only a few will have seen the real dangers inherent in a form of rule that could develop into a tyranny (Tacitus underestimates the opposition but he gives an excellent impression of the gradual growth of Augustus' power). For most people the immediate advantages were more than adequate to stifle doubts.

In fact, what must have been most worrying during the years immediately following the battle of Actium in 31 B.C. was the fear that Augustus would last no longer than his predecessors in the struggles for power: the downfall of Augustus was synonymous with civil war.[2] But Augustus, who must have spent the previous

[1] A further important factor is the existence of volunteer armies, who took an oath to a specific general and depended on him for a satisfactory termination to their service (see Smith, op. cit. 33 ff.).

[2] Horace expresses this idea several times: see, for instance, ode 24, and commentary below.

decade in thinking and planning, made swift progress. First, in the military field he returned to Romans their taste for victory with a triple triumph of his own in 29 B.C., and then successes in Spain and Illyria. It was a shrewd instinct that made him surround himself with an aura of military success: the shame of recent defeats was an important political consideration. Secondly, and with a rashness that shows how deeply committed he was to the programme, he seems to have started on a very extensive series of social reforms in 28 B.C.: these reforms were designed to encourage marriage and penalize adultery, not simply to increase the birth-rate but also to inculcate a new standard of morality that did not rate personal and momentary pleasure above the interests of the state. These reforms were rejected, and this rejection must have brought a moment of serious danger when it would have taken little to bring down the regime. It was a risk which Augustus took, but he persevered and passed some of the laws in 18 B.C. and the rest in A.D. 9. With these reforms should be reckoned others which concerned religion and education—particularly physical education that would rear a youth ready for the rigours of military service.[1] Thirdly, he consolidated his own position, and, especially, by a clever political manoeuvre, he 'restored the Republic' in 27 B.C. With the born politician's instinct for the best use of the right words, he did not abdicate like Sulla, but manipulated the constitution to suit his style of government and then called it the Republic (so Tacitus speaks of him 'presenting himself as consul' and—probably after 23 B.C.—as 'satisfied with the *tribunicia potestas*'). But this is a judgement that the hindsight of two millennia allows one to make —and it expresses the reality far too crudely; yet very few at the time will have been in a position to analyse the events which they saw in such a way as to expose the inner reality. There is no reason to regard Augustan poets as being insincere because they celebrate the consolidation of Augustus' rule and the resurgence of Roman military glory, and deplore the failure of his moral legislation.

In Republican times social and political influence found expression in the patron–client system; the members of the ruling oligarchy formed the social plateau and their influence penetrated downwards

---

[1] See p. 35 below, n. 2.

by a chain reaction into all layers of society. Agreement (even in competition) at the top meant a peaceful and stable society: dissension at the top meant anarchy and often mob rule through wide regions of society. When Augustus came to power he created a new and single centre of gravity in society from which all lines of influence radiated outwards; the formation and refinement of this system was a gradual process, but consciously planned from the beginning as a means by which Octavian the party-leader became Augustus the head of state and the Julian faction merged into the Roman state. Augustus collected men of all sorts and talents round him. Earlier Republican oligarchs had done the same sort of thing—though on nothing like the scale of Augustus—but he seems to have been the first both to realize the importance of literature to the politician and to have been in a position to gather all the greatest poets of the time round him. He achieved this through Maecenas, who was clearly an excellent judge of literature and selected his poets with impressive accuracy; that this patronage was neither oppressive nor demanding must have been due to a number of reasons—the antiquity of the system, the awful warning presented by the writings of Greek panegyrists, and (not least) the sense that the Roman state really was taking an important and inspiring new turn. The system worked, to judge by the results, and poets were involved, as they had never been before, in the reality of actual and contemporary politics.

3. THE POET AND THE COMMUNITY

Greeks and Romans were puzzled, as we are from time to time, about the nature of poetry and its function and what the poet is supposed to be doing. There had been a time when these questions were not puzzling. Romans could look back to a time in early Greece when Homer, composing epic poetry, was the story-teller of his people, the historian who preserved the past traditions of the race and who combined entertainment with instruction when he recited. Hesiod could be seen to perform an equally important function as a repository of technical knowledge. The lyric poets wrote their poems for performance on specific social occasions like drinking-parties, celebrations of various sorts such as that held for a returning victor at the games, hymns to be sung at temples during religious festivals, and many more. In Athens during the fifth century, comedies and tragedies were written for performance at specific festivals. In all this, an account could be given of poetic activity which related the poet directly to the society in which he lived. But gradually, during the fourth and third centuries, the social occasions which, by their very nature, instigated poetic activity, died away and a new phenomenon appeared: the scholar-poet who worked as a literary expert in a great library like that at Alexandria and wrote poetry as a mere part of his activity. These poets took a step which was decisive for later poetry: they continued to write the same sort of poetry as earlier poets had done, but, instead of having real social occasions for which their poems were designed, they treated the occasions as part of the imaginative structure of their poems. So they wrote hymns without any thought of a religious performance; they wrote drinking-songs without parties in prospect; they wrote epitaphs without any idea of having them inscribed on a tombstone. That is, the imagined occasion supplied the form for the poem and sometimes suggested the outline of the thematic treatment. A number of the odes in Book iii appear to be prayers: for instance, 13, 18, 21, 22, 25, and, to some extent, 11, 26, and 30; in some of these, especially 21, the actual formal elements of a prayer are quite evident, but they are to be regarded as purely of literary, not of liturgical, significance. The form enables the poet to give appropriate treatment to the main ideas which he has in mind. Equally, a number of the odes are built around the concept of a party and prescribe or describe or anticipate its pleasures: for instance, 8, 14, 17, 19, 21, 28, and 29. Here, too, the idea of a particular type of party gives the poet an opportunity for expressing a certain range of ideas that traditionally centre on such a social occasion. Another antique form to be seen in *Odes* iii is the παρα-κλαυσίθυρον or serenade: the lover is outside his mistress's house and reproaches her for excluding him. What Horace has done in *Odes* iii. 10 is to use the form to accommodate some new ideas of his own that superimpose Roman concepts on the traditional Greek material. The consequence of this is of the utmost importance for understanding

Horace's lyric poetry: the critical reader must be prepared to regard the form of the poem and sometimes those elements which condition the form (such as the setting) as a modification of traditional material to suit the poet's immediate inspiration, and to realize that the poet's own ideas may well lie some considerable distance behind this outward structure. A special feature of this which is widespread in Horatian lyric is easy to grasp: Horace normally represents himself as singing his poetry, often to the accompaniment of the lyre; this is a pure fiction, derived from the fact that the early Greek lyric poets whom he most immediately used as his models, like Sappho and Alcaeus, wrote their poetry for musical performance.

The features so far examined go some way to establishing a distinction between form (which is often an adaptation of tradition) on the one hand and content (which contains the substance of the poet's immediate inspiration) on the other. From the same Greek background there emerges another distinction which is important for Roman poetry. Is poetry entertaining or useful? Does it teach as well as divert? When Plato decided that poets should be expelled from his ideal Republic, it was largely because he thought that they entertained men with falsehood and by arousing undesirable emotions. Aristotle met the two objections with his theories of imitation and catharsis: poets simply indulged a particular form of the universal human tendency to imitation, and, so far from arousing undesirable emotions, they provided a perfectly devised outlet for them. But such arguments were on far too high a theoretical plane to have a practical impact on the making or understanding of poetry. Poets— and their readers—returned to the simple contrast of usefulness and entertainment. The great Hellenistic poets seem mainly to have regarded poetry as pleasurable and not useful. In Rome the distinction came to a sharp focus in the poetry of Catullus. For the early writers of epic, Naevius and Ennius, the history of Rome had been established as the most sublime subject-matter for epic poetry. Yet not only does Catullus sneer directly at such poetry (for instance at the *annales Volusi* in poem 36), but his only references to the affairs of Rome are, with negligible exceptions, scabrous lampoons on eminent men. It is not that Catullus' poetry is not at times really serious; it is that nothing is further from its intention than to be educational or didactic. Contemporaries like Cicero and Lucretius took a much more serious view of the function of poetry, and Cicero composed poems on the great historical events in which he had taken part. Yet both Cicero and Lucretius are, in different ways, old-fashioned and, poetically, Augustan poets stand much closer to Catullus. What happened between Catullus and the Augustans is obscure, but it can be expressed by saying that the later poets were totally committed politically. This was probably not entirely due to Octavian; there seems to have been a tendency (which can be seen in Virgil's *Eclogues*) for poets to find some of their themes in the absorbingly serious events of contemporary politics, and Octavian (with Maecenas' help) probably seized on and developed this tendency.

At any rate a serious political commitment is the leading characteristic of Augustan poetry, and of no earlier poetry. Of course, in earlier times poetry was written in praise of great men like Scipio or Marius, but it was panegyrical poetry written by men who were financially dependent on the patrons whom they praised. Most poets had patrons whom they addressed: it was a convention. But when Catullus addresses Cornelius Nepos in poem 1, it is in a casual, off-hand way that shows no sort of dependence on him whatever. The great Augustan poets do address their patrons: Maecenas and, later, Augustus. But there is nothing of panegyric in their poetry; the way in which they speak of politics is not to invent virtues in their patrons and praise their great deeds, but to take a serious analytical interest in contemporary society and its ills. They all had reason to feel gratitude to Augustus: by an interesting co-incidence, Virgil, Horace, and Propertius all seem to have lost their estates in the confiscations. This fact, no doubt, provided a lever for patronage; but this patronage was not like the close financial dependence on an individual of earlier times: this was more like state patronage, and its gentle stimulus is evident in the very different approaches made to political questions by the three poets mentioned. There is no sense of a dictated party line. But in the end this problem becomes one of literary criticism: how successful are the political odes as poems?

In considering this question several further facts need notice. The range of Horace's *Odes* is astonishingly wide: some are humorous, in the manner of Mr. John Betjeman, others are deeply serious. This is a range of tone. But there is an equally wide range of subject-matter: the *Odes* are a wonderfully varied collection of poetry. Here an important distinction is relevant. Horace is often contrasted unfavourably with Catullus as a lyric poet: briefly, Horace lacks the immediacy and personality of Catullus. There is a misunderstanding here, because Horace was not trying to write the same sort of poetry. Catullus wrote, for the most part, from a strictly autobiographical point of view: the character who appears in his poetry is Gaius Valerius Catullus. But Quintus Horatius Flaccus does not appear in the *Odes*. If we want to find him, he is to be sought in the *Satires* and *Epistles*; these are the poetic forms in which he expressed a strictly autobiographical point of view. In the *Odes* he speaks, as most Greek and Roman poets spoke, not in his own private character but in his character as an inspired poet. At one end of the scale this gives that pleasantly ironic detachment to his love poetry; at the other, it gives the high prophetic tone to much of his political poetry. The ordinary individual citizen, Quintus Horatius Flaccus, could not speak in the tones of the opening to *Odes* iii. 1. The person who speaks there is (3) *Musarum sacerdos*, and this represents a term which Augustan poets, with the new sense of the high seriousness that could belong to poetic activity, resurrected and refurbished to describe their activity: this was the word *vates*, which had sunk to meaning something like 'fortune-teller' or 'oracle-monger', but Augustan poets used it to express what they, in contradistinction to Catullus, felt to be a part of the poet's function—his duty to speak out in high tones on the great issues of contemporary society. He achieved this high function in virtue of that vision which was not granted to ordinary men, but which was symbolized in the poet's relationship with the Muses and which we call inspiration—a phenomenon which the ancient world recognized, but which they found as hard to explain as we do. Horace tries to convey an impression of it in *Odes* iii. 25.

4. STYLE

Understanding of poetry will be inadequate unless there is some attempt at critical assessment, but this needs criteria which are sensitive to the poet's intention and which take into account the conditions under which he was writing. They must be capable of being applied not only to the technical features of language, vocabulary, and metre but also to the ideas which are being expressed and especially to the connection of thought. In what follows some criteria are suggested and illustrated which are intended to help in the critical assessment of Horace, *Odes* iii, and also in appreciating the poet's intention. Neither the criteria nor the illustrations have the slightest pretence to be exhaustive and readers will be able to think of others for themselves.

Originality was important to Horace and he makes a number of claims to it. For instance, in odes 1. 2–4 and 25. 7–8 he claims an originality of subject-matter which is justified in virtue of the fact that he was composing a new type of poetry on political themes (see pp. 9-10). In ode 30. 13–14 he claims to be the first to transfer the poetry of Sappho and Alcaeus into Latin, and in *Epistles* i. 19 (well worth reading in this context) he expands this claim and explains the nature of the originality involved. But all these claims are to an originality which is relative to the work of other poets; what needs consideration by the reader of the *Odes* is the way he achieved originality in the actual process of writing single poems. There are several ways in which this can be regarded.

A. *Originality as avoidance of the ordinary and commonplace*

This sounds negative, but that is only because it is easier to define what the poet is trying to avoid than what he succeeds in attaining. To find means of expression which convey a sense of novelty and immediacy is a basic poetic aim, and is most easily demonstrated in technicalities of language.

1. *Language.* Here Horace is very successful. The danger in this is that desire for novelty will create a bizarre and artificial style. It is worth comparing the technique of Horace and Virgil in this respect with that of Catullus, for instance, in poem 64. There

Catullus cannot escape censure for artificiality since he crowds novelties of linguistic and metrical form one on top of another, constantly repeating features like spondaic endings and a separation of adjective and noun that encloses the metrical unit[1] until they come near to seeming like tricks. He is only saved by the brilliance and variety of his invention. Neither Horace nor Virgil makes the mistake of using any linguistic device often; in fact, both are masters of a technique whereby the occasional use of a particular linguistic device is yet made to create a positive impression on the reader. Both display an extremely fine literary tact in this respect and neither could be accused, as Johnson accused Milton (with exaggeration and unfairness):

> The truth is that, both in prose and verse, he had formed his style by a perverse and pedantic principle. He was desirous to use English words with a foreign idiom. This in all his prose is discovered and condemned; for there judgment operates freely, neither softened by the beauty nor awed by the dignity of his thoughts; but such is the power of his poetry, that his call is obeyed without resistance, the reader feels himself in captivity to a higher and nobler mind, and criticism sinks in admiration.

Italian, and especially Latin, idioms are clear in Milton; Horace creates an impression of novelty by applying Greek idioms to Latin. Here is a brief analysis of this and other ways in which Horace creates linguistic novelty.

(a) *Greek usages*: 8. 13–14 *amici . . . sospitis* (cf. 19. 9–11 *lunae . . . novae, noctis mediae, auguris Murenae*), 17. 16 *operum solutis*, 27. 69–70 *abstineto . . . irarum*, 27. 67 *perfidum ridens*, 30. 11–12 *agrestium regnavit populorum*.

(b) *archaisms*: 5. 38 *duello* (cf. 14. 18), 7. 4 *fide* (genitive), 2. 29 *Diespiter*.

(c) *novel forms of expression*: the infinitive used to limit the sphere of an adjective on which it depends (as in 11. 3–4 *resonare . . . callida*, 3. 50 *spernere fortior*, 12. 11 *celer . . . excipere*, 29. 50 *ludere pertinax*); 5. 42 *capitis minor*;[2] 8. 25 *neglegens ne . . .* (the novelty of the construction is mitigated here by the fact that *ne* may also be

---

[1] See G. Williams, *Tradition and Originality in Roman Poetry*, 705 f.
[2] See p. 58 below.

taken as governed by *cavere*): the construction, together with the comparative detachment of the participle, underlines the humorous tone in which so unexpected a word is used of Maecenas.

(*d*) *combined novelty of language and thought*: here are some phrases where it is difficult to say whether their originality is more linguistic or conceptual—2. 1 *amice pauperiem pati*, 6. 24 *de tenero . . . ungui*, 14. 11 *iam virum expertae*, 16. 30–2 *segetis certa fides meae . . . fallit sorte beatior*. Others can be added to this list, but it is no coincidence that editors at various times have attempted to emend all these phrases; it is this sort of originality that is most vulnerable to regularizing interpretation.

What is remarkable here is the difficulty which a reader has in identifying and categorizing linguistic peculiarities; relatively few— and those widely scattered—can be pointed out, yet the total effect is of the forging of a linguistic means of expression which is new and peculiar to Horace. What Johnson says of Milton is here applicable: 'Through all his greater works there prevails a uniform peculiarity of diction, a mode and cast of expression, which bears little resemblance to that of any former writer, and which is so far removed from common use that an unlearned reader, when he first opens his book, finds himself surprised by a new language.' To this effect in Horace word-order contributes its part and something will be said of this below (*Style* D).

II. *Ideas*. There is a criticism often made of Horace that his ideas and subject-matter are hackneyed, mere reflections on life and love and death and the pleasures of the moment, eked out with Greek mythological decoration. No criticism could be sillier—as if a man could find more important or worth-while topics on which to reflect. Johnson was a hostile critic of Gray's poetry (and his criticism is well worth consideration by the reader of Horace), yet he ends his essay on Gray with these words:

In the character of his Elegy I rejoice to concur with the common reader; for by the common sense of readers uncorrupted with literary prejudices, after all the refinements of subtilty and the dogmatism of learning, must be finally decided all claim to poetical honours. The *Churchyard* abounds with images which find a mirror in every mind, and with sentiments to which every bosom returns an echo. The four stanzas beginning 'Yet even these bones' are to me original: I have never seen the notions in any other place; yet he that reads them here, persuades himself that he has always felt them. Had Gray written often thus, it had been vain to blame, and use-less to praise him.

The matter could not be better put. The reader of Horace often feels that he is on familiar ground; yet, when he looks closer, the attempt to find sources or analogies in earlier literature reveals that he was mistaken. In the past this discovery has often led to violent attempts to emend Horace into conformity with earlier writers. It is to be hoped that those days have gone. The most familiar source of ideas for Greek and Roman writers was Greek mythology; yet even here the familiar becomes unfamiliar as the reader senses an attitude in the poet to this material which conceals unexplored depths. For instance, in ode 4. 42 ff. he introduces the battle of the Giants against the Gods with the words *scimus ut*. . . . But what does he mean by saying 'we know how . . .'? He has just been addressing the Muses: does he mean more than 'poets have related how . . .'? The tone of the words is vital (and must be connected with *testis mearum . . . sententiarum* in 69–70—on which see *Style* C III below). The poet turns out to be using the legend as a political parable which he never explains, and the poem ends with the lover Pirithous—nothing to do with the Giants. Horace never uses Greek mythology—as contemporaries like Propertius did—at face value: the poet's attitude and tone always intervene between the reader and the familiar material.[1] This is clear, for in-stance, in the poetic use to which he puts the great 'text' of ode 1 (5–8), when it is related to its Greek background. A similar novelty becomes clear in poems which deal with religious topics. Ancient religion—especially Roman—is agreed to have been related to the due performance of clearly prescribed acts; yet it is hard to read odes like 13, 18, 22, or 23, without becoming aware of an under-lying emotion that goes some way to expressing a spiritual content associated, for the poet, with the ritual acts. Again, in ode 24, Horace takes Scythian communism and gives it an entirely new

---

[1] See further *Style* D II.

orientation; this is historically false, but it carries conviction within the poet's view of contemporary Roman society so that its factual basis becomes irrelevant: it is an imaginative creation in its own right.

B. *Originality as the defeat of expectation*

To a poet predictability is an enemy: the expected must be avoided. Or, to look at it the other way round, a poet fails to the extent that the reader can predict the movement of his thoughts. Horace generally defeats expectation, constantly achieves the effect of literary surprise (which is independent of the reader's knowledge of what is coming, so that the surprise is capable of re-creation with each re-reading). Here are some of the ways in which it is achieved.

I. *Syntactical means.* 16. 1–7 . . . *munierant* . . . *si non* . . . *risissent*; here the device of using the 'vivid' construction (indicative for subjunctive) is made more effective by placing the apodosis before the protasis. In 14. 14–15 *nec tumultum nec mori per vim metuam*, the noun and the infinitive are parallel, which means that the infinitive is substantival; *mori per vim* means 'violent death' but the unexpectedness of the structure is evident from the number of commentators who try to compare ode 9. 11 (where *mori* is true infinitive). In ode 14. 14–15 the poet creates an elegant variation with an element of linguistic surprise.

II. *Structural variation.* A linguistic structure consisting of a series of parallel clauses (especially with anaphora) creates expectation of its own continuity and so provides the poet with an opportunity to defeat expectation. Horace makes admirable use of this. In ode 8. 13–16 there are three clauses, each with verbs in the imperative, of which the first two are connected with *et* but the third stands in asyndeton: *sume . . . et . . . perfer . . . : . . . esto . . .* Here the first two verbs give specific instructions, but the third indicates a more general circumstance (rather than ordering Maecenas to produce it). In the same ode 25–8, two more imperative verbs are linked by *et* while the final *linque severa* stands in asyndeton: here too the final instruction is more general and ends the poem with the force of a general maxim. There is a perfect example of the same thing in ode

18. 5–8: here the two pre-conditions for the sacrifice are linked by (6) *nec*, but the third statement stands in asyndeton and is set apart from the others and the direct force of (5) *si*: *vetus ara multo fumat odore*. The effect of this is to move the ideas forward to the second half of the poem where the festival is described as if it were actually happening: in 7–8 the poet has the altar smoking. In ode 4. 73 ff. the poet describes the miseries that followed the violence of the Giants in three clauses linked by *nec* (75 and 77), but a final clause follows in asyndeton 79–80 *amatorem trecentae Pirithoum cohibent catenae*: the structure is perfectly adapted to introduce the surprise-figure of Pirithous and to end the poem with the example of un-ending vengeance that punishes the gentle violence of an attractive character.

III. *Parenthesis*. This is an excellent way of introducing an idea as if it occurred to the poet on the spur of the moment. In 3. 9–16 there is a clearly defined structure of parallel clauses with anaphora of *hac* (there is an internal variation in 13 where Bacchus is addressed in the vocative and *tuae tigres* becomes the subject); this sequence is broken by a parenthesis in 11–12 where a surprising (and potentially awkward) vision occurs to the poet of Augustus in heaven. Here the parenthesis serves to convey the surprising suddenness and incon-sequentiality of the vision, and insulates the poet from a crude desire to flatter. At 11. 1–2 the parenthesis is deliberately used to underline the hymnic character of the opening. In 17. 2–9 a monstrous paren-thesis contains the main (joking) point of the poem, but suggests that it occurred to the poet on the spur of the moment.

IV. *Surprise openings*. These need no detailed demonstration. It is a constant feature of Horace's composition that he begins his odes on a note that excites interest in the reader and gives him no ready clue to the main content of the poem. Horace is a master of the indirect and unexpected approach.

V. *Unexpected movement of ideas*. This too needs no detailed illustra-tion: there is a constant surprise in the movement of ideas in Horace's *Odes*. For instance, in ode 1, the great 'text' of 5–8 gives no hint of the way in which it is related to the ideas that follow; the reader must wait till he has completed the ode. In 2. 6 ff. the poet introduces the figure of the queen and then of her daughter, but, unexpectedly, he drops the queen from consideration and concentrates on the daughter because her romantic situation best accommodates his concept of the young Augustan. This characteristic can be seen from another point of view in the considerable thematic complexity of the *Odes* which elevates them into major poetic forms, often closer to the range of Pindaric composition than to the delicate structures of Alcaeus and Sappho.

C. *Changes of tone*

Two facts are vital for appreciation: not only did Horace regard the *Odes* as a highly personal poetic form but also Romans always read aloud. This meant that a poet could count on a far greater sensitivity to tonal changes in readers who were accustomed, as a natural part of the basic process of reading, to discern tones of voice in written words. Horace exploited this possibility with great skill. What follows simply picks out a few ways in which tonal changes were made.

I. *Humour.* Some poems are humorous through and through; these, like ode 26, are easy enough to discern, but the danger in such cases is rather that in the poet's self-mockery the capacity of this attitude in Horace's hands to conceal an underlying element of seriousness will be missed. This could easily happen in the case of odes 21 or 28, perhaps even of ode 9. Easier to miss, however, is the sudden flash of humour in a serious context, such as the fish in 1. 33–4 or Faunus' unsuccessful love-affairs in 18. 1, or the sudden picture of the poet literally wrapping up in the philosopher's cloak of virtue or marrying that honest (but unattractive) bride, Poverty, in 29. 54–6. What is remarkable in all such cases is that the flash of humour does not in the least disrupt the general seriousness of the context. The reason lies in the mobility of the poet's tone in which a real, vivid personality finds expression.

II. *Tonal complexity.* Corresponding to the thematic complexity of the *Odes* (see *Style* B v) is a complexity of emotional tone. It is clear, for instance, in ode 13 where tonal responses to changes of theme are particularly subtle. One of these changes is characteristically produced by dropping the single word *frustra* (6) which halts the flow of ideas and shifts it into a new channel (similarly with *frustra* in 7. 21 where the word leads to powerful assertion of the young man's constancy and, accordingly, prepares for the suggestion of the girl's vulnerability). This constant interaction and movement of tone and theme and emotion is an outstanding characteristic of Horace's poetical composition.

III. *So-called 'prosaic' words.* An insensitivity has been detected in Horace which led him to include in the vocabulary of his *Odes* a large element of prosaic words whose unpoetical quality is demonstrated by the fact that they were not used by other Roman poets. The interpretation rests on a number of false assumptions about 'poetic diction' in Roman poetry,[1] but the underlying facts are worth attention and do need explanation. Some examples are significant: for instance, *atqui* is judged unpoetic, yet Horace uses it at odes 5. 49 and 7. 9; curiously enough *quod si* escapes such censure, yet Horace uses it in a very similar way at ode 1. 41. What is significant here is that at all three points there is a distinct change of tone and the poet marks this by the weighty particle (which functions much as *frustra* at 7. 21 and 13. 6). The tone of words is vital in such highly wrought poetry. One way of classifying words is to place them on a scale which extends from pure emotional expression at one extreme to sheer factual description at the other: 'poetic' words will tend to the former extreme, 'scientific' to the latter. Some words, judged prosaic in Horace, tend to the latter extreme. For instance, in ode 5. 53 *negotia* is most unusual in poetry, but it is its factual, descriptive, unemotional tone that is so effective in 5. 53 (and in 29. 49). So, too, in 5. 14 *condicionibus* and *dissentientis* are both judged prosaic, but both (apart from the powerful two-word line which they construct) create a factual assessment of Regulus' stand that is distinct from the emotional rhetoric alike of what precedes and what follows. In ode 4. 69–70, *testis mearum* . . . *sententiarum* sounds prosaic: rather it is factual and serves the vital purpose of insulating the poet's thought from the conventional 'poetic' material with which he illustrates it and draws the reader into understanding that there is a concrete political reality, unstated but hinted at in the preceding stanza (65–8). Consideration of the

[1] For details, see G. Williams, *Tradition and Originality*, 743 ff.

tonal aspect of words is essential: it is quite unimportant that other poets do not use *strenuus* (28. 3), but essential for the humour of the ode that the word is a soldier's expression of approval; *cena* is unusual in poetry, but the important fact for understanding ode 29. 15 is that Horace is envisaging a potentially real situation—his poem is constructed round the idea that Maecenas really will come to 'dinner' (naturally Virgil does not talk of Aeneas having 'dinner'). Much of the subtlety of Horace's *Odes* lies in the poet's sensitivity to the tones of words and their capacity to convey tonal implications without further assistance. There is endless material for the reader to consider here.

D. *Imagination and Interpretation*

It is one of the most attractive features of Horace's *Odes* that the reader is required to co-operate imaginatively with the poet: it is, as it were, only when the reader's imagination is fitted to the evidence which is the poem that the latter becomes complete and intelligible. There are several ways in which Horace achieves this result.

I. *Dramatic monologue.* In the *Odes* the poet speaks so that each poem is essentially a monologue by the poet. But often the poem has a complex dramatic setting and, though only the poet speaks, other characters participate. Horace developed a most satisfying technique for the composition of such poetry whereby the dramatic setting is not described but is left for the reader to construct imaginatively from clues casually dropped in the course of the monologue. This technique has no place in the reflective and philosophical poems; so it characterizes ode 8, but not ode 29 which is also to Maecenas. It is absent from odes 1–6, 16, and 24, but it is clear in 7, 8, 9, 10, 12, 13, 14, 15, 17, 18, 19, 21, 23, 26, and 28. (See the commentaries on these poems.) In some of them it is only quite a small effort of imagination that is demanded of the reader as in 9 or 13 or 15; but in some much is required, as in 19 or 23 or 26.

II. *Demand on the reader's knowledge.* Corresponding to the technique of dramatic monologue there is, in the reflective and narrative poems, a demand for knowledge on the reader's part who must apply that knowledge in the required way. Characteristic of this demand is the way in which the poet often avoids description of a political situation: he allows a faint outline of a real political situation to begin to appear and then sheers off into more traditional poetic material. The reader is required not only to recognize the political situation but also to grasp the relationship of the traditional material to it. This is especially striking in ode 4 where the situation is only touched on in the most general terms; then the reader is required to understand the relationship of the ode to Pindar's *Pythian* i and from this relationship construct the political thoughts which concern the poet. Similar to this is the poet's attitude to the traditional material derived from Greek mythology: the reader's knowledge of this is assumed and the poet feels free to use the material at will, leaving his own attitude to be inferred and applied by the reader to understanding the poem. This is particularly subtle and complex in the reinterpretation of the Europa-myth in ode 27.

III. *The blending of Greek and Roman.* Horace sets his *Odes* in a world of the imagination which is neither directly Greek (though there are Greek names and many other features of Greek culture) nor completely Roman (though major elements in the setting of every poem are Roman). This means that elements from real contemporary life stand in the poems on the same level as literary elements derived from the Greek (and Roman) past. So, for instance, Faunus in ode 18 has a touch of Pan about him, or Diana in 22 has something of Artemis, or the young man Hebrus in ode 12 is in some respects a young Augustan, or in ode 19 the party, though Greek in major respects, yet celebrates the augurship of Murena. The poet delights in the fact that he can thereby allow the real world to appear fleetingly every now and again behind and in this world of imagination: it gives the opportunity for a similar subtlety of technique as he applies in his treatment of politics (see II above).

E. *Ornamentation*

There is hardly anything in the *Odes* that can be called mere ornamentation: ode 16. 1–8 is most unusual in that every noun has an adjective (most of them merely ornamental) which is placed

next to it. But the title is a convenient label under which to gather a
series of scattered observations on features in Horace's use of words.
They are rightly scattered and incomplete—a mere indication to a
reader who will be able to notice many more for himself—since
it is a particular virtue of Horace's writing that there is no mechanical
application of a series of formulae. It is mainly his word-order that
needs notice here,[1] because it is endlessly various and inventive.
He can write 11. 35–6 *et in omne virgo nobilis aevum* or 13. 9 *flagrantis
atrox hora Caniculae* or 14. 5 *unico gaudens mulier marito* where a
noun and adjective in agreement enclose a similar pair, but in the
first example the two pairs are chiastically arranged, in the latter
two they are in parallel. At another time he writes 3. 19–20 *fatalis
incestusque iudex et mulier peregrina* or 4. 33–4 *Britannos hospitibus
feros et laetum equino sanguine Concanum*, both of which are chiastically
arranged structures of noun and adjective set in series. Sometimes
the noun and adjective enclose a syntactical unit as in 3. 37–8 *longus
inter saeviat Ilion Romamque pontus* or 43–4 *triumphatisque possit Roma
ferox dare iura Medis* or 4. 7–8 *amoenae quos et aquae subeunt et aurae*.
Or a series of nouns and adjectives may be interlaced as in 3. 29–30
nostris ductum seditionibus bellum or 4. 2 *regina longum Calliope melos*
or 24. 40–1 *horrida callidi . . . aequora navitae*. A particular feature
(found more often in Virgil's *Eclogues*) is the placing of an apposi-
tional phrase round the noun which it qualifies as in 24. 42 *magnum
pauperies opprobrium*. There are endless observations of this sort to
be made and the fact is that even structures which look at first
sight the same are really distinct (most of those quoted above as
similar can easily be distinguished from one another). The important
feature of Horace's word-order is the way in which the poet succeeds
in combining what seem to be opposites: extreme elegance of
arrangement with a sense of ease and naturalness; there is little
that is forced or artificial in the writing of the *Odes*.

It is surprising how little there is of the great formal stylistic
ornaments of simile and metaphor. The great simile of the Tiber
in ode 29. 33–41 is very unusual; it is more in Horace's character
that in 20. 1 ff., where he is clearly thinking of a Homeric simile, he

---

[1] On the complex question of rhyme, see O. Skutsch, *Bull. Lond. Inst. Class. Stud.*
11 (1964), 73–8.

abandons the form of the simile and uses the name 'lioness' directly of the woman. In the same way, metaphor is not conspicuous in the *Odes*. The result is that the style is much more homogeneous and the reader is made more aware of the force of individual words than in a style where the fireworks are impressive and the gaps between less noteworthy. It is in the choice of individual words that Horace is supreme: in 22. 5 *imminens* by itself creates a perfect thumb-nail sketch of the hill farm-house and (7) *obliquum* exactly hits off the young boar—even for a reader who knows nothing whatever of the creature. So too in 17. 7 *innantem* is perfect for the river spreading out over the marshy valley, or, in 21. 20 *apices* fixes on a startling detail that brings alive a totally alien scene. But there is endless material here too for the alert reader of Horace.

Of rhetorical tricks there is nothing: Horace values irony and understatement; such writers have little use for the artillery of rhetoric. It is entirely characteristic that repetition, analogous to what is called epanalepsis in other writers, is only used by Horace in the speeches attributed to others—and then it is used with extreme discretion: Regulus is made to say in 5. 21 . . . *vidi*; *vidi* . . . but a clause ends between the two words. Under the same conditions Juno says in 3. 60–1 . . . *Troiae*; *Troiae*. . . . When she begins her speech with (18) *Ilion Ilion* . . ., the repetition gives life to her reluctant abandonment of hatred and to a heavy warning tone. In all his writing Horace avoids excess, cultivates subtlety and precision.

F. *Structure in the Odes*

There is nothing mechanical about the structural patterns of individual odes (a simple balance of structure as in ode 20 is unusual), but a few general features are worth pointing out.

I. *Ring-composition*. A number of odes are so constructed that they end by returning to a modified form of the theme with which they began; so 1, 13, 15, 19, 20, and 24. This is a neat solution for the difficulty (to which Horace had various solutions) of bringing a short poem to a convincing conclusion.

II. *Odes with an uneven number of stanzas*. Many odes which consist of an uneven number of stanzas are constructed on a pattern by which two blocks of sense are linked by a single intervening stanza. The two blocks of sense are usually equal (so in 8, 10, 14, and 11—if the stanza 25-8 is genuine), but, as in ode 16, need not be.

III. *Epigram-form*. A number of odes are so constructed that they are modelled on Greek epigrams, but by an increase of the thematic and emotional complexity the poet has upgraded the tiny epigram into a major poetic form: this applies to 7, 10, 13, 15, 17, 20, 22 and 26.[1]

IV. *Groups of stanzas*: this is—naturally enough—Horace's normal method of construction. A sequence of similar groups as, for instance, in ode 1 (where the groups contrast with one another) or in ode 29 (where each group is made up of two internally contrasting stanzas) is unusual. The difference between groups of stanzas is sometimes a change in point of view as in 5. 41-8 contrasted with 49-56 or in 4. 42-8 as contrasted with 49-64 (see commentaries on both odes). It is often difficult to see the structural demarcations simply because Horace's movements of thought are neither obvious nor pedagogically signalled by the poet. The *Odes* are, in general, a highly intellectual form of poetic composition.

G. *Structure of the Book of Odes iii*

There is little that needs saying on this. Horace clearly collected the first six so-called 'Roman Odes' at the beginning both because of their community of topic and because of the importance of political poetry in his odes (for his view see ode 25). At the beginning of the second half of the book (i.e. ode 16) he set an ode addressed to Maecenas, whom he also honoured by setting another ode addressed to him not at the end of the book (a position which had to be reserved for the Epilogue, ode 30) but immediately before the end. Otherwise variations or similarities of subject-matter or metre have dictated the order of poems and, while some plausible reasons for particular collocations may be guessed at, it is a waste of time to speculate on a matter of which the poet himself probably had no clear idea and which, in any case, has minimal literary relevance.

[1] It is worth contrasting these poems with the Greek epigrams collected in the Appendix.

5. METRES

This is only an outline sketch of the metres used by Horace in *Odes* iii.

I. *Alcaic*

– – ∪ – –   – ∪ ∪ – ∪–
Odi profanum vulgus et arceo;
∪ –∪ – –   – ∪ ∪ –   ∪∪
favete linguis: carmina non prius
– –∪ – – –   ∪ – –
audita Musarum sacerdos
– ∪ ∪ –   ∪∪–   ∪ – –
virginibus puerisque canto.

used in odes 1–6, 17, 21, 23, 26, 29.

II. *Sapphic*

– ∪– – –   ∪ ∪ –   ∪ – –
Martiis caelebs quid agam Kalendis,
– ∪– – – ∪ ∪ – ∪ – –
quid velint flores et acerra turis
– ∪ – – – ∪ ∪–   ∪ –   –
plena miraris positusque carbo in
– ∪∪ – –
caespite vivo

used in odes 8, 11, 14, 18, 20, 22, 27.

III. *Asclepiadic rhythms.* There are a number of varieties of this system, but all are marked by the occurrence of the combination – ∪ ∪ – surrounded by other combinations of syllables (mostly spondee – – to begin and iambus ∪ – to end).

– – – ∪ ∪– ∪–
(*a*) festo quid potius die
– – – – ∪∪– –   ∪∪ – ∪ –
(*b*) quid fles Asterie quem tibi candidi
– – – ∪ ∪––
(*c*) Thyna merce beatum
– – – ∪ ∪ –   ∪–
(*d*) constantis iuvenem fide

Odes 7 and 13 are written in stanzas of (*b*), (*b*), (*c*), (*d*).
Odes 9, 15, 19, 24, 25, 28 are written in stanzas of (*a*), (*b*), (*a*), (*b*).

Ode 10 and 16 are written in stanzas of (*b*), (*b*), (*b*), (*a*).
Odes 30 is written in stanzas of (*b*), (*b*), (*b*), (*b*).

IV. *Ionic a minore*. This consists of the unit ᵕᵕ – – repeated and division into lines is arbitrary, but the following is a convenient arrangement consisting of three-line stanzas (only ode 12 is written in the system):

> ᵕᵕ –   – ᵕ   ᵕ – – ᵕᵕ – –   ᵕ ᵕ   – –
> Miserarum est neque amori dare ludum neque dulci
> ᵕᵕ – – ᵕᵕ   – – ᵕᵕ – –   ᵕᵕ– –
> mala vino lavere, aut exanimari metuentis
> ᵕ ᵕ– – ᵕᵕ –   –
> patruae verbera linguae.

FURTHER READING

BOWRA, C. M., *Greek lyric poetry*, Oxford, 2nd ed. 1961.
— —-*Pindar*, Oxford, 1964.
FRAENKEL, E., *Horace*, Oxford, 1957.
GOW, J., Q. *Horati Flacci carmina*, Cambridge, 1906 (often reprinted).
PAGE, D. L., *Sappho and Alcaeus*, Oxford, 1955.
RAVEN, D. A., *Latin metre*, London, 1967.
SYME, R., *The Roman revolution*, Oxford, 1939.
WEST, D., *Reading Horace*, Edinburgh, 1967.
WILKINSON, L. P., *Horace and his lyric poetry*, Cambridge, 2nd ed. 1951.
WILLIAMS, G., *Tradition and originality in Roman poetry*, Oxford, 1968.

1

Odi profanum vulgus et arceo:
favete linguis; carmina non prius
   audita Musarum sacerdos
      virginibus puerisque canto.

regum timendorum in proprios greges,   5
reges in ipsos imperium est Iovis,
   clari Giganteo triumpho,
      cuncta supercilio moventis.

est ut viro vir latius ordinet
arbusta sulcis, hic generosior   10
   descendat in Campum petitor,
      moribus hic meliorque fama

contendat, illi turba clientium
sit maior: aequa lege Necessitas
   sortitur insignis et imos,   15
      omne capax movet urna nomen.

destrictus ensis cui super impia
cervice pendet, non Siculae dapes
   dulcem elaborabunt saporem,
      non avium citharaeque cantus   20

somnum reducent: somnus agrestium
lenis virorum non humilis domos
   fastidit umbrosamque ripam,
      non Zephyris agitata Tempe.

desiderantem quod satis est neque   25
tumultuosum sollicitat mare
    nec saevus Arcturi cadentis
        impetus aut orientis Haedi,

non verberatae grandine vineae
fundusque mendax, arbore nunc aquas   30
    culpante, nunc torrentia agros
        sidera, nunc hiemes iniquas.

contracta pisces aequora sentiunt
iactis in altum molibus; huc frequens
    caementa demittit redemptor   35
        cum famulis dominusque terrae

fastidiosus: sed Timor et Minae
scandunt eodem quo dominus, neque
    decedit aerata triremi et
        post equitem sedet atra Cura.   40

quodsi dolentem nec Phrygius lapis
nec purpurarum sidere clarior
    delenit usus nec Falerna
        vitis Achaemeniumque costum,

cur invidendis postibus et novo   45
sublime ritu moliar atrium?
    cur valle permutem Sabina
        divitias operosiores?

'I despise the uninitiated mob and I warn them off: keep your tongues
well-omened; I, priest of the Muses, am singing songs, never heard
before, to girls and boys.

'The rule of dread kings is over their own flocks (5), over kings
themselves is the rule of Juppiter, famed for his triumph over the
Giants, moving all things by his nod.

'It happens that one man lays out his vine-trees more spaciously in their furrows than another, that this man descends to the Campus Martius a candidate of nobler blood (11), that this man contends with an advantage in character and reputation, that that man has a larger crowd of followers: with impartial law Necessity chooses by lot both high and low (15), her capacious urn holds every name.

'For the man over whose impious neck a drawn sword hangs, Sicilian feasts, though elaborate, will not produce a pleasurable taste, the music of birds and the lyre (20) will not bring back sleep: gentle sleep does not despise the humble homes of country folk nor a shady bank nor a valley fanned by west winds.

'If a man desires what is sufficient, neither (25) a stormy sea makes him anxious nor the savage onset of setting Arcturus or of the rising Kid, nor his vineyards being beaten down by hail or his farm cheating as the tree puts the blame now on rains (30), now on stars scorching up the fields, now on storms out of season.

'The fish feel their waters contract as piles are driven down into the deep; at this point many a contractor (35) with his slaves, and the owner who is bored with the land, shoot down building-rubble: but Fear and Forebodings climb as high as the owner, and black worry does not abandon the brass-plated yacht and squats behind the rider (40).

'But if neither Phrygian marble nor the wearing of purple brighter than a star nor Falernian wine and Persian balsam soothe a man who is troubled, why ever should I labour to erect a hall raised high on pillars to be envied and in a modern style (46)? Why ever should I exchange my Sabine valley for more troublesome riches?'

The poem opens with a stanza (1–4) in which a particular type of announcement is made: this was the announcement by the priest who officiated at the ceremonies of a mystery religion (such as Orphism or that at Eleusis), warning the uninitiated to remove themselves and those present to avoid ill-omened words (virtually a request for silence).[1] What makes this announcement totally different from any real example is the emphasis on the personality of the announcer. Then in line 3 it becomes clear that this is no ordinary priest, but a 'priest of the Muses', i.e. a poet (for whom Augustan poets resurrected the ancient religious word *vates*, which had over the previous two centuries degenerated to meaning 'oracle-monger'[2]). It is a proud announcement, in the manner of an announcement at the

---

[1] See also ode 14. 11, p. 93 below.   [2] See p. 10 above.

mysteries, by which the poet declares first those whom he does not address (the general mass of the people), then his chosen audience (boys and girls) —the representatives of a new generation: this choice of audience prepares the reader for a certain didactic element in the poetry. Finally, the poems will be totally original (2–3): the poet is conscious that no one has ever yet brought poetry directly into the field of contemporary politics.[1]

There follows, in equally elevated tones, a great generalization (5–8): kings may be the greatest creatures on earth, but they are subject to Juppiter. The relation of this to the poem as a whole will be discussed below, but the alien nature of the political system on which the generalization depends is clear: the kings and tyrants of the Hellenistic East (cf. pp. 116–7).

The next two stanzas (9–16) depict the great men of the Roman world: the landowner with more property than other men, then candidates for election to magistracies, each with his own advantage of birth (10), character and reputation (12), or influence (13–14). These are the greatest men Rome knows, yet, like everyone else, they are subject to the ordinances of Death (*Necessitas*)[2] which show neither fear nor favour.

A contrast follows in the next two stanzas (17–24): first the Sicilian tyrant of Syracuse (430–367 B.C.), Dionysius who, flattered by Damocles, invited him to dinner but in the middle of the meal drew his attention to a sword suspended by a hair over his guest's head. Such was the life which Damocles flattered, and the poet recalls the incident in (18) *non Siculae dapes*[3] . . . but goes on to draw out the point which interests him more: neither the songs of birds (Romans were fond of aviaries) nor music of the lyre will help such men as Dionysius to sleep. This motif forms the bridge to the contrasting picture of the poor countryman's house, the shady bank, and the valley stirred by the west wind (the time of year is spring and the valley is given the generic name of that most famous of all valleys, Tempe in Thessaly).

The picture of ideal country life brings the poet's thoughts (25–32) to a favourite theme—that of the contented man (the spiritual analogue to the ideal described in 21–4). Such a man who wants a mere sufficiency is not worried by sea-storms at the end of October when Arcturus set and the Kid rises (the reason is that he is not trying desperately to get rich by trading overseas, with his ships at sea right till the moment when winter storms start);[4] nor does he fear failure of his crops with the young vines

---

[1] See pp. 9–10 above.

[2] See ode 24. 6, p. 125 below.

[3] The poet concentrates his thoughts on Damocles, but his real target is the tyrant Dionysius; Damocles is only the means of revealing the inner nature of the tyrant's life.

[4] Like Gyges in ode 7, p. 69 below.

battered by hail, the farm cheating him (by not giving due returns on seed), and his orchard sterile, blaming rain, drought, and storms.[1]

A totally contrasted picture follows (33–40) of the rich Roman, bored with the land (36–7 *terrae fastidiosus*), and building his luxury villa out into the sea.[2] But, however high he goes (in wealth or building), fear and forebodings (*Minae*) go as high; and, though he engages in the rich man's pursuits of yachting (his yacht is decorated with brass plates) or riding, black depression never leaves him.

Finally the poet bursts out impatiently[3] (41–8): but if all the trappings of wealth do not help a man when he is sick at heart (*dolentem*), why should I build an enormous house, or exchange my Sabine valley for a wealth that only brings more worry with it?

The problem in this poem concerns the relationship of the great generalization (5–8) to the rest. Though it is often said that the first stanza (1–4) is separate from the poem, was added later, and intended to introduce *Odes* iii. 1–6, yet the stanza is integral in the sense that it provides a personal opening which is picked up by the equally personal ending (41–8), so that the poem, as a whole, shows a characteristic form of 'ring-composition'.[4] But the tone of the two personal passages is on a higher, more solemn level than is usual for Horace, so the generalization (5–8) comes in appropriately on the same level. Its function is to take the greatest men the world knows and show that they, in turn, are subordinate. It is doubly significant that the poet chooses a non-Roman category of being; for this both universalizes the statement more thoroughly in insulating it from things Roman and also allows the poet to draw on a famous passage from Callimachus' *Hymn to Zeus* where it is said that kings belong to Zeus alone.[5] The statement collects added literary authority from the great Hellenistic poet. The form of the statement is exactly mirrored in the next two stanzas (9–16): a dramatic movement of ideas brings in the great men of the Roman world, followed by the force which levels them with other men—Death. Then the poet's ideas move out again to collect a strange non-Roman example—a Sicilian tyrant; here the movement of ideas changes, because he is not shown to have a leveller (or superior) but to have a flaw in his life which makes an individual at the other end of the social scale (21–4) his superior. Here the movement of

---

[1] The reason why this man, paradoxically, does not fear such terrible disasters is that he is not a landowner trying to amass the considerable wealth which farmers could make. Perhaps the poet pictures his ideal man as a shepherd, contented with little.

[2] The straight-faced flash of humour in the picture of the fish sensing their kingdom contracting is characteristic of Horace and does not disrupt the seriousness of the context: cf. ode 18. 1 (p. 106 below) and see *Style* C 1.

[3] On the force of *quodsi*, see *Style* C III.   [4] See *Style* F 1.   [5] See Appendix, no. 4.

ideas has changed from being an alternation from upper to lower to being an oscillation between contrasts. So from the ideal of simple country life, the poet moves to the ideal of the self-sufficient man and his freedom from the worries produced by ambition (25–32). This introduces a new psychological element into the contrasts, and so the poet's thought naturally moves to the ambitious self-seeking Roman, a wonderfully concrete picture; yet he too is assailed by doubts and fears and the sinister black figure that sits behind the rider. On this note of worry (41) the poet enters in his own person with indignant questions that set the ambitious ideal of wealth (and all it can buy and build) on one side, and the quiet ideal (with echoes of the country life in *valle . . . Sabina*) on the other. Thus what happens in this poem is that the poet begins with the most elevated of relationships (that between kings and Juppiter) and then he transposes the contrasted elements in a series of movements that have two effects: first, they reduce the terms on both sides so that finally the poet himself can appear on one side; secondly, they modify the controlling relationship between the contrasted elements so that, though it starts as a fundamental ordinance of the universe (the hierarchy of kings and Zeus, then Death), it comes to be a psychological factor identifiable with ambition on the one side and contentment on the other. Looking back from the end of the poem, the reader sees that the thought in the poet's mind was, basically: 'What is the point of personal ambition?' But, though the essence of the poet's thought can be formulated in a way that sounds didactic, there is nothing moralizing about the poem: it is reflective and prophetic in tone. The ideas come not as moral propositions clothed in rhetorical expression, but as a series of concrete and sharply contrasting pictures. The poet allows the basic moral to lose its own identity and function simply as an underlying principle which, as the reader can see on reflection, serves to organize the stream of images in the poet's mind. The poem has another great merit: it moves in unexpected and unpredictable ways, following no hackneyed train of thought but keeping the reader guessing to the end, and preserving something of the sense of things unsaid that characterizes great poetry.

2

Angustam amice pauperiem pati
robustus acri militia puer
    condiscat et Parthos feroces
        vexet eques metuendus hasta

vitamque sub divo et trepidis agat 5
in rebus. illum ex moenibus hosticis
    matrona bellantis tyranni
        prospiciens et adulta virgo

suspiret, eheu, ne rudis agminum
sponsus lacessat regius asperum 10
    tactu leonem, quem cruenta
        per medias rapit ira caedis.

dulce et decorum est pro patria mori:
mors et fugacem persequitur virum,
    nec parcit imbellis iuventae 15
        poplitibus timidove tergo.

Virtus repulsae nescia sordidae
intaminatis fulget honoribus,
    nec sumit aut ponit securis
        arbitrio popularis aurae; 20

Virtus, recludens immeritis mori
caelum, negata temptat iter via,
    coetusque vulgaris et udam
        spernit humum fugiente penna.

est et fideli tuta silentio 25
merces: vetabo, qui Cereris sacrum
    vulgarit arcanae, sub isdem
        sit trabibus fragilemque mecum

solvat phaselon; saepe Diespiter
neglectus incesto addidit integrum; 30
    raro antecedentem scelestum
        deseruit pede Poena claudo.

'Let the sturdy boy learn through hard military service to suffer
pinching poverty as a friend and let him harass the ferocious Parthians,

a horseman to be feared for his spear, and let him spend his life under the open sky and in dangerous (5) circumstances. Let the wife of the warring tyrant, looking at him from enemy walls, and (with her) let her grown-up daughter sigh—ah!—lest her royal betrothed, inexperienced in battle, should provoke that lion dangerous (10) to touch whom bloodthirsty rage drives through the middle of the carnage.

'Desirable and glorious is a death for one's country: death follows even after the man who runs away and does not spare the knees and timid back of a spiritless youth (16).

'Virtue, knowing no disgrace in defeat at the polls, shines with untarnishable honours and does not take up or put down the axes (of office) at the whim of popular favour (20); virtue that opens up heaven to those undeserving to die explores a route along a path (usually) denied, and disdains the vulgar mobs and the damp earth with escaping wing.

'There is also a sure reward for reliable silence (25): I shall not allow the man who has published the rite of secret Ceres to be under the same roof-beams or to cast loose a frail boat in my company; often the Sky-Father, when ignored, has coupled an innocent with a guilty man (30); seldom has Vengeance abandoned a wicked man through lameness of foot though he has got a start on her.'

The poem opens with a surprising idea: the ideal Augustan young man is to treat poverty as a friend. Two facts need mention here: many earlier writers (especially Greeks) personified poverty (Horace treats her as a bride in 29. 55-6), and *paupertas* and *pauper* do not connote the idea of 'poverty' and 'poor', since they signify only a relative indigence and this is a condition to be approved morally (suggesting hard work and absence of selfish ambition).[1] It becomes clear in the next words that the poet is thinking of the spiritual advantages which this condition offers the campaigning soldier (it is the condition which produced great military glories in the far past—6. 33 ff.). An Augustan youth can have no greater purpose than to prepare himself for the crusade against the Parthians, which so obsessed Romans mindful of several defeats but especially of the humiliation in 53 B.C. Acclimatization to poverty will help him to live rough (*sub divo*, 'under the open sky', recalls the Indo-European Sky-God),[2] and in constant

---

[1] The idea is to be expressed not so much as the intrinsic virtue of poverty, but as the moral advantage conferred by absence of wealth and ambition. The idea appealed to Horace: it is the basis of odes 1, 16, and 24; but it is sometimes simply assumed (see ode 15. 1, p. 96 below).   [2] See p. 36, n. 2 below.

danger (5–6). What follows is a surprising view of the young Augustan, from the enemy's point of view; but it is a romantic point of view which recalls, above all, the famous scene in the *Iliad* where the ladies of Troy look out over the battlefield and pick out the heroes on both sides (iii. 146 ff.). The poet mentions the enemy queen but concentrates on the princess[1] who watches her betrothed, fearful lest he, a tiro in war, may fall in with the young Augustan, who is like a lion. It is a curious scene, which has no connection with contemporary realities either in the general situation depicted or in the singling out of the young Augustan (since he would, presumably, be accompanied by thousands like him).[2]

In this first section (1–12) the poet has been exhorting. With the famous generalization (13) he seems to fall into a reflection which is not directly based on what he has been saying, but which, as often happens with generalizations in Horace, moves the flow of ideas into a different channel: the basic moral principle for which men fight. It is noble—and even attractive—to die for one's country—and in any case, even if one runs away, one only gets killed. There is a curiously unpoetical realism about the qualification in 14–16 (that is never quoted on memorials on which line 13 appears). This will be judged to be bathos and the transitional nature of the stanza will be missed unless its effect is analysed. The effect is not merely to state negatively what is asserted in the generalization (13), but to make plain that the man who shows cowardice loses everything—even his life. The basic idea is that in certain situations a man's life is forfeit anyway and then it is for him to exploit that fact positively.

Such exploitation is *virtus* and so this transitional stanza moves the flow of ideas into a more abstract channel. The poet now reflects (17–20) that *virtus* does not consist in satisfying personal ambition by election to political office: such election—or failure to win election—has nothing to do with *virtus* (expressed by saying that failure means loss of reputation but *virtus* can know nothing of that since it is not *virtus* which holds political office); election is a matter of fickle popularity, changeful as the wind (20 *popularis*

---

[1] See *Style* B. v.

[2] The thoughts which underlie this opening section of the ode are related to Augustus' interest in the education and training of the young. Augustus revived the practice whereby boys of good family joined youth clubs (*collegia iuvenum*) and went through training in physical exercise and horsemanship. Probably at the age of seventeen they went into the *Juventus* to train seriously as soldiers. The emphasis on individualism which Horace creates here may reflect the aristocratic bias of this youth-movement, and the Homeric scene may come more readily to the poet's mind because the intricate and dangerous display which the youth put on was called the *Lusus Troiae* (cf. Virgil, *Aeneid* v. 548–74). For details see H. Last in *Cambridge Ancient History*, x. 462–4.

aurae). Immortality, the poet continues, is denied to man (so the path to it is denied—*negata . . . via*), but the aim of *virtus* is to attempt a journey (22 *temptat iter*) along that route and open it up for those who deserve to live (*immeritis mori*). In this way it leaves the great masses of men behind and soars into the fiery firmament[1] (in contrast with which the earth is damp—*udam . . . humum*).

The poet's thoughts again take an unexpected turn: even if a man does not attain such heights, there is still a sure reward for devoted silence. Then, as in 14–16 he does not define *dulce et decorum* positively, so here too he moves out into an extensive negative definition, instead, of the punishment for failure to keep silence. This is expressed in the form of an analogy: the poet expresses his own repugnance for the man who has revealed the mysteries of Ceres or Demeter (the most famous centre was at Eleusis) and ends with a statement of the inevitability of punishment. The poet will not be under the same roof with such a man (lest it fall on them both) or in the same ship (lest it sink), for Juppiter's punishment has often involved the innocent with the guilty (29). It is a solemn and foreboding warning emphasized by the archaism *Diespiter* (Juppiter was, in origin, a sky-god or god of the daylight)[2] and by the personification of *Poena* as if she were one of the Furies (who pursued, for instance, Orestes).

This is a puzzling poem, and it is not made easier by the fact that it has an undefinable relationship to one or more poems of the Greek lyric poet Simonides. Line 14 clearly translates ὁ δ' αὖ θάνατος κίχε καὶ τὸν φυγόμαχον (Simonides fr. 19 Page), and 25–6 is based on ἔστι καὶ σιγᾶς ἀκίνδυνον γέρας (fr. 77 Page) which is reported by Plutarch (*reg. et. imp. apophth.* 207 c) as a favourite saying of Augustus. There are other, less close, possible echoes of Simonides, and, in suggesting a roof falling in and a ship sinking, Horace may be alluding to two miraculous escapes of Simonides from certain death. A very ingenious reconstruction has been made, on the basis of this poem of Horace, of an ode of Simonides on civic virtue.[3] This can hardly help with Horace; for it is scarcely conceivable that Horace simply translated Simonides, even less that he made the understanding of his ode dependent on the recognition that it was a simple translation and that its relevance was to be found in the context of Simonides' poem. So Horace's

---

[1] Cf. ode 3. 10 *arces . . . igneas*.

[2] The name Juppiter is formed from the vocative **Dieu-pater* and is etymologically related to Sanskrit *Dyaus*, Thraco-Phrygian Διως and Δεως, Greek Ζεύς, Messapian Δειπατυρος. The god was a sky-god and so responsible for weather; in particular, thunder and lightning were his weapons.

[3] By W. J. Oates, *The Influence of Simonides of Ceos upon Horace*, Princeton, 1932,

poem must have a meaning in its own right. It is notable that Horace has added the word *fideli* to the phrase of Simonides: so the silence becomes one that can be relied upon—by whom? In the context it can only be by the Roman state and especially by Augustus. If so, what does the poet mean? The poem clearly comes under the rubric of the first ode (1–4) and is addressed to the younger generation. The older generation were far from silent when Augustus tried to introduce moral reforms and they succeeded in getting them rejected.[1] At first sight it seems as if the poet refers to the sort of silence that consists in keeping a secret, but that is only because he goes on to consider a particular type of blabbing tongue which can be set inside a traditional framework[2] and permit the poet an imaginative movement outwards into thoughts about the fundamental moral structure of the universe: a perfect ending to the poem, and one which echoes—in its reference to the Mysteries—the opening of ode 1. This is a poetic complex of ideas that should not be allowed to narrow the concept of silence. A political interpretation of the poet's praise of silence fits the movement of the poem. For it opens with concrete thoughts on military service (1–6) and (rather in the way that silence is illustrated by an excursion into religious mysteries) this is illustrated by an excursion back into Homeric epic (6–12). Then the poet reflects on the virtue of courage which is a basic essential, but in a way that makes it easily appear as a part of a wider concept of *virtus* (13–16). This wider concept is examined (17–24) and very significant stress is laid on its independence of the people as a whole and their ideas. This implicit rejection of the mass echoes the theme with which ode 1 opened and it appears again in odes 3 and 24: the context is usually one of opposition to beneficial but unpopular action or actions, and it is hard not to recognize an allusion to the rejection of Augustus' moral reforms. So that background is suggested here in 17–24. Then, just as courage was treated as a part of *virtus*, so, from the wider concept of *virtus*, the poet concentrates on what he regards as another part of it, *fidele silentium*. This, by the poetical stratagem of defining a special case of it negatively in terms of the punishment for its contravention, he succeeds in setting in the widest possible context of a fundamental moral law. So the ideas move from honest poverty to soldierly qualities, to bravery, to patriotism, to virtue that faces opposition, to the trusty silence that acquiesces in what is right but unpopular.

---

[1] See p. 5 above. The theme is clear also in odes 6 and 24 (see commentary on these).

[2] The technique here is to allow a political situation just to begin to appear and then to steer instantly away into remote, though analogous, concepts. See p. 42 below. Consequently, to understand the opening idea solely by reference to the concepts which follow it is to fall into a basic error.

3

Iustum et tenacem propositi virum
non civium ardor prava iubentium,
   non vultus instantis tyranni
      mente quatit solida neque Auster,

dux inquieti turbidus Hadriae,   5
nec fulminantis magna manus Iovis:
   si fractus illabatur orbis,
      impavidum ferient ruinae.

hac arte Pollux et vagus Hercules
enisus arces attigit igneas   10
   (quos inter Augustus recumbens
      purpureo bibet ore nectar);

hac te merentem, Bacche pater, tuae
vexere tigres indocili iugum
   collo trahentes; hac Quirinus   15
      Martis equis Acheronta fugit,

gratum elocuta consiliantibus
Iunone divis: 'Ilion, Ilion
   fatalis incestusque iudex
      et mulier peregrina vertit   20

in pulverem, ex quo destituit deos
mercede pacta Laomedon, mihi
   castaeque damnatum Minervae
      cum populo et duce fraudulento.

iam nec Lacaenae splendet adulterae   25
famosus hospes nec Priami domus
   periura pugnaces Achivos
      Hectoreis opibus refringit,

nostrisque ductum seditionibus
bellum resedit: protinus et gravis   30
    iras et invisum nepotem,
        Troica quem peperit sacerdos,

Marti redonabo; illum ego lucidas
inire sedes, ducere nectaris
    sucos et adscribi quietis   35
        ordinibus patiar deorum.

dum longus inter saeviat Ilion
Romamque pontus, qualibet exsules
    in parte regnanto beati;
        dum Priami Paridisque busto   40

insultet armentum et catulos ferae
celent inultae, stet Capitolium
    fulgens triumphatisque possit
        Roma ferox dare iura Medis.

horrenda late nomen in ultimas   45
extendat oras, qua medius liquor
    secernit Europen ab Afro,
        qua tumidus rigat arva Nilus.

aurum irrepertum et sic melius situm,
cum terra celat, spernere fortior   50
    quam cogere humanos in usus
        omne sacrum rapiente dextra,

quicumque mundo terminus obstitit,
hunc tanget armis, visere gestiens,
    qua parte debacchentur ignes,   55
        qua nebulae pluviique rores.

sed bellicosis fata Quiritibus
hac lege dico, ne nimium pii
rebusque fidentes avitae
tecta velint reparare Troiae;   60

Troiae renascens alite lugubri
fortuna tristi clade iterabitur,
ducente victrices catervas
coniuge me Iovis et sorore.

ter si resurgat murus aeneus   65
auctore Phoebo, ter pereat meis
excisus Argivis, ter uxor
capta virum puerosque ploret.'

non hoc iocosae conveniet lyrae:
quo, Musa, tendis? desine pervicax   70
referre sermones deorum et
magna modis tenuare parvis.

'The man who is just and tenacious of his purpose neither the anger
of his citizens bidding him do what is wrong nor the face of a
threatening tyrant shakes from his solid determination, nor the south
wind, wild emperor of the restless Adriatic (5), nor the mighty hand
of thundering Juppiter: if the world should fall shattered, the ruins
will strike him unafraid.

'By this virtue Pollux and the roaming Hercules strove and
attained the fiery citadels (10), (amongst whom Augustus shall
recline and drink nectar with rosy lips); your tigers carried you,
meritorious through this virtue, father Bacchus, drawing the yoke
with indocile necks; by this virtue Romulus (15) escaped Acheron,
(drawn) by the horses of Mars, when Juno spoke a word that found
favour with the gods in council:

' "Ilion, Ilion a doomed and corrupt judge and a foreign woman
turned (20) into dust—Ilion condemned by me and the chaste
Minerva, along with its people and fraudulent king ever since he,
Laomedon, cheated the gods of the agreed payment. Now for the
Spartan adulteress no longer shines (25) her infamous guest nor does

the perjured house of Priam any longer beat back the warrior Greeks with Hector's help, and the war, prolonged by our own quarrelling, has died away (30): henceforth I shall forgive Mars both the grievous causes of my anger and that hated grandson whom the Trojan priestess bore; him I shall permit to enter the bright abodes, to drink the juices of nectar, and to be enrolled among the peaceful (35) ranks of the gods.

' "As long as the sea rages wide between Ilion and Rome, let the exiles happily hold sway in whatever region they please; as long as the herd leaps over the tomb of Priam and of Paris (40) and wild beasts conceal their young there with impunity, let the Capitol stand gleaming and let fierce Rome have the power to dictate terms to the conquered Medes. Feared everywhere, let her extend her name to the uttermost (45) shores, where the midway water separates Europe from Africa, where the swollen Nile irrigates the fields.

' "Stronger to despise[1] gold, undiscovered and thus better situated when the earth conceals it (50), than to compel to human use everything sacred with rapacious hand, whatever limit is set to the world, this she shall touch with her weapons, eager to go and see in what part the fires rage wildly (55), or in what part mists and rainy dews.

' "But I tell their fortune to the warlike people of Rome on the condition, that they do not, over-dutifully and over-confident in their luck, seek to rebuild the houses of ancestral Troy (60); the fortune of Troy, reborn under an evil omen, shall be treated once again with grim disaster, as I, wife and sister of Juppiter, lead the troops to victory. Should its wall rise again three times in brass (65) with the assistance of Phoebus, three times let it fall, cut down by my Argives, three times let the captive wife wail for her husband and sons."

'This will not suit my humorous lyre! Whither, Muse, are you going? Cease wilfully (70) to recall speeches of gods and demean great themes by a humble style.'

The ode opens with a general definition of a man who is both just and determined in the face of opposition. It would be hard not to connect this with the two stanzas (17–24) on *virtus* in the previous ode—the more so because both passages treat opposition in terms of the mass of the people. The presumption that Augustus is to be seen behind the generalizing terms

---

[1] On *spernere fortior*, see *Style* A 1 (c).

is confirmed by the mention of him in 11–12. But two characteristic features of Horace's writing are to be noted: first, Augustus is not connected explicitly with the generalization; he is only associated with Pollux and Hercules who are explicitly connected with it. Secondly, no sooner has the poet allowed a first glimpse of a real contemporary political situation to appear in the first two lines than he moves away to an alien political system (converting the just man into one of the ruled instead of a ruler) and then further away to natural phenomena, finally (7–8) to a picture of the whole world falling in ruins. He seems to avoid explicit re-creation of a real political situation; he allows it to begin to appear, then, as it were, draws poetical red-herrings across the trail. So in ode 2 he creates a picture of the real Roman army and its Parthian enemy (1–4), but instantly moves away to a remote Homeric scene (5–12); at the end the theme of silence and its political importance begins to appear (25–6), but the poet instantly sheers off into a remote analogy from the mysteries. In ode 4, he allows Augustus and his attitude to appear (37–42) but moves straight into a Pindaric parable of the Giants; in ode 24, he refers to Augustus and his aims in 25–32, but puts all this in such a generalizing form as to conceal it as one of many similar situations in human history.

Here the opening generalization comes to an end, and a series of examples occurs to the poet of heroes who attained immortality through justice and constancy: Pollux and Hercules, both benefactors of mankind, occur first and the poet casually remarks that Augustus will drink nectar with them—implying that it will be for the same reason. He goes on to name Bacchus and Romulus (or Quirinus, son of Mars): all are benefactors of mankind, and Horace—who never treats Augustus as divine—confers on him a sort of deification by association several times, as here, by putting his name among those of these very heroes. The specific detail of his 'crimson lips' (whether this refers to the quality of eternal youth or—more likely since it would have a relevance mentioned with the act of drinking—the staining of his lips by nectar)[1] seems an error of taste and judgement. The poet now

---

[1] Athenaeus (*deipnosophistae* xiii. 604 A–B) explains that such expressions are possible in poetry and quotes Simonides (frag. 80 Page) πορφυρέου ἀπὸ στόματος | ἰεῖσα φωνὰν παρθένος, describing a girl 'speaking with crimson lips'; this is usually taken to support the idea that Horace refers to the concept of eternal youth. It does not—unless the παρθένος is a goddess. But, since nectar was thought to have the power to confer immortality (see p. 43, n. 1 below), Horace may be combining the concepts of youth and immortality in the concrete detail of crimsoned lips. At *Aeneid* ii. 593 Aeneas describes Venus as speaking *roseo . . . ore*. There is nothing to be said for the present tense (12) *bibit* (offered by more than half the manuscripts): it would only suggest that the poet (with prophetic insight) could see this happening now. On the parenthesis, see *Style* B III.

tells of the chariot, drawn by tigers, which carried Bacchus to heaven, and
of how the chariot of Mars, his father, took Romulus, but, as he mentions
that name, the whole circumstance of Romulus' entry into heaven comes to
his mind, as if it were by accident. The great speech of Juno on that occasion
occupies the next 50 lines or so.

The first part of her speech shows how she came to allow Romulus into
heaven (18–36). She recalls her hatred of Troy which goes back beyond the
judgement of Paris (18–21) to Laomedon's fraud on Apollo and Neptune
(21–4). She now recalls how all that is over—Helen and Paris (25–6),
Priam's great house defended by Hector (26–8), the war prolonged by
quarrels among the gods who took different sides (29–30). This reflection
motivates her forgiving Mars her grievances against him (the usual
meaning of the plural *irae*), especially his son by Ilia (30–3). She will
allow Romulus to be enrolled among the gods (*adscribi* is the technical
term for enrolling a new citizen) and to drink nectar (*ducere* must be the
right word, not *discere*—as if there were vintages of nectar—since it is the
act of drinking that marks the god).[1]

The second part of her speech leaves Romulus and surveys the future of
Rome in three sections, the first and last of three stanzas each (37–48 and
57–68), thematically connected, and a centre section of two stanzas (49–56).
The first section declares the conditions for Roman survival (38–9) and
greatness (42–8); it is in splendidly impressive language, with evocative
pictures of the site of Troy deserted except by wild animals amid the tombs
of Priam and Paris. She chooses the Capitol as the symbol of Rome (42–3)
and the Parthians as enemies that need to be defeated (43–4); Rome may
extend her sway to the straits of Gibraltar (46–7) and to the Nile (48).
This section is permissive: if Rome fulfils certain conditions, she is permitted
to become the greatest power in the world. But it is the centre section which
foretells Rome's greatness as the power that will extend her control to the
ends of the earth (53–4); and she will do this, eager to find out what the
unknown parts of the world are like (54–6). What is denied implicitly in
this assertion of motive is that conquest will be carried out for mere gain.
An analogous assertion led Juno to the prophecy: she states that Rome is
braver at rejecting gold (better left hidden in the earth) than at snatching
everything—including sacred things—with the one thought of human

---

[1] The manuscripts divide more or less equally between *discere* and *ducere*. Quite
apart from the absurdity of the picture created by *discere*, the verb *ducere* has a special
point: the food and drink of the gods was supposed of itself to confer immortality on
those who partook of them (*Iliad* v. 341–2, Pindar, *Olympians* i. 60 ff.). The mis-
taken word *discere* could easily arise if the hasta of the *-u-* in *ducere* was crookedly
and carelessly written to produce the appearance of *-is-*.

advantage (49–52). This moral viewpoint is not stated as a condition for world-conquest, but to explain how the Romans will be able to accomplish it. The necessity of disregarding wealth is a theme in which Horace often finds inspiration, and the Romans themselves were convinced that an important factor in their superiority over other nations was their piety.[1] The effect of this point of view expressed here is to allow to the Romans the credit for their successes, which do not come automatically, by fate, if Romans observe certain rules laid down by Juno, but are won by them in virtue of their own high moral character. In the final section of her speech (57–68), Juno comes back explicitly to the one condition which enables her to declare a great future for Rome: Romans must not rebuild Troy; if they do, it will simply fall again, for Troy has a different *fortuna* from that of Rome[2] (61–2).

Here the poet breaks in, as it were, on his inspiration and asks his Muse what she is up to: this theme will not suit his playful style (*iocosae . . . lyrae*)—such topics as speeches of gods are subjects for epic. This stanza has an obvious function as a conclusion to the poem, and Horace uses the device also, for instance, at *Odes* ii. 1. 37–40. But the effect here is more complex. The future tense *conveniet* is a neat device which concludes the poem, without, however, casting any reflection back over it; it is only if such inspiration continues that it will become unsuitable. But the effect of the stanza is also to dissociate the poet from a personal involvement in the themes of the poem. Horace never himself goes surety for the truth and reality of mythological and miraculous events. In *Odes* ii. 19 he claims to have seen Dionysus, but he adds *credite posteri* ('believe me, later generations'), a sophisticated device whereby he asks readers to share a poetic attitude (but in *Odes* iii. 25, where he speaks of his own sensation of inspiration using the god as a symbol and his rites as an analogy, he does not need to dissociate himself). At 11. 17–20, the subjunctives turn the details into a report.[3] In 16. 1–8 he uses the legend of Danaë for an ulterior purpose and does not pledge support for its truth. In 27 he gives the legend of Europa a highly sophisticated treatment which does not involve making poetry out of the truth of its traditional features. In *Odes* i. 2. 1–20 he relates the prodigies in

---

[1] Cicero expresses the idea strikingly in *de natura deorum* ii. 8 and examples from many writers, both Greek and Roman, of the same concept are collected by A. S. Pease in his notes on the passage.

[2] This expression is based on a concept that developed in Hellenistic times: each city was supposed to have its own Fortune, its Τύχη, which personified the city and was often represented by a female statue. The *Fortuna* of Troy was naturally sinister and tragic.

[3] See p. 84 below.

a style that absolves him from personal commitment. In ode 3 he dissociates himself in two ways: first, the inspiration was imposed on him and he protests as soon as he can recover his wits; secondly, the theme is that of epic[1] and so both the treatment and the details are to be viewed as belonging to a different genre of poetry. This latter consideration not only requires the reader to see the whole concept of gods in council as a piece of epic machinery, but it applies this same consideration to the means by which the poet constructed the council-scene: in particular, it asks that the prophetic picture of Augustus (11–12) should be regarded as a conventional epic device. Horace's reason for dissociating himself personally in all these poems is that he is a lyric poet, writing personal poetry; fiction is one thing, but traditional mythical material needs an ulterior purpose if it is to find a place in personal poetry—epic is the genre which treats such material for its own sake.

This is a complex poem and it may seem that there is no connection between the opening and the speech of Juno. But the speech is introduced with great artistry (like the story of the Danaids in 11): the poet lists a series of heroes who won immortality and, as he mentions the last name, the curious circumstances of his entry into heaven occur to him.[2] Another important link is between the praise of (Augustus') constancy in the face of opposition (1–8) and the moral virtues which Juno attributes to Rome (49–52), for it was to establish similar virtues that Augustus promulgated his moral legislation and incurred hostility. But the link also consists in the sense of Rome's destiny as world-ruler so powerfully expressed by Juno, for this was an ideal that Augustan Rome was coming to value again. Juno's speech can be viewed as a sort of answer to a problem raised by the contemporary epic, the *Aeneid*: how and when did Juno's hostility to Rome cease? The speech is a counterpart to the great speech of Juppiter in *Aeneid* i. 257 ff. Too little attention is often paid to this aspect of the speech and too much to Juno's warnings against rebuilding Troy. Suetonius reports (*Jul. Caes.* 79. 3) rumours that Julius Caesar at one time planned to shift the capital eastwards to Alexandria or Troy. There is small reason to think it more than rumour, still less to credit the modern suggestion that Augustus was reviving the plan and Horace warning against it. The fact is that the poet uses this warning of Juno's as the motivation for her change of attitude to Rome: he makes her focus her hostility on Troy—but Troy is destroyed,

[1] This is the real meaning of saying that it will not suit the lyre which symbolizes his own lyric, and of characterizing the subject-matter as speeches of gods (frequent in epic).

[2] On the impression of inspired 'randomness' created by such connections of thought, see *Style* B III.

the Romans have no interest in it now, and they must not think of rebuild-
ing it (57–68). The goddess has been generous and the poet must be allowed
to construct a speech for her that would not make nonsense to a reader of the
Aeneid.[1]

4

Descende caelo et dic age tibia
regina longum Calliope melos,
   seu voce nunc mavis acuta,
      seu fidibus citharave Phoebi.

auditis, an me ludit amabilis   5
insania? audire et videor pios
   errare per lucos, amoenae
      quos et aquae subeunt et aurae.

me fabulosae Vulture in Apulo
nutricis extra limina Pulliae   10
   ludo fatigatumque somno
      fronde nova puerum palumbes

texere, mirum quod foret omnibus,
quicumque celsae nidum Acherontiae
   saltusque Bantinos et arvum   15
      pingue tenent humilis Forenti,

ut tuto ab atris corpore viperis
dormirem et ursis, ut premerer sacra
   lauroque collataque myrto,
      non sine dis animosus infans.   20

vester, Camenae, vester in arduos
tollor Sabinos, seu mihi frigidum
   Praeneste seu Tibur supinum
      seu liquidae placuere Baiae.

[1] See, on this, Fraenkel, *Horace* 267–9.

vestris amicum fontibus et choris   25
non me Philippis versa acies retro,
    devota non exstinxit arbos,
      nec Sicula Palinurus unda.

utcumque mecum vos eritis, libens
insanientem navita Bosphorum   30
    temptabo et urentis harenas
      litoris Assyrii viator,

visam Britannos hospitibus feros
et laetum equino sanguine Concanum,
    visam pharetratos Gelonos   35
      et Scythicum inviolatus amnem.

vos Caesarem altum, militia simul
fessas cohortis abdidit oppidis,
    finire quaerentem labores
      Pierio recreatis antro;   40

vos lene consilium et datis et dato
gaudetis almae. scimus ut impios
    Titanas immanemque turbam
      fulmine sustulerit caduco,

qui terram inertem, qui mare temperat   45
ventosum, et urbes regnaque tristia
    divosque mortalisque turmas
      imperio regit unus aequo.

magnum illa terrorem intulerat Iovi
fidens iuventus horrida bracchiis   50
    fratresque tendentes opaco
      Pelion imposuisse Olympo.

sed quid Typhoeus et validus Mimas,
aut quid minaci Porphyrion statu,
    quid Rhoetus evulsisque truncis   55
        Enceladus iaculator audax

contra sonantem Palladis aegida
possent ruentes? hinc avidus stetit
    Vulcanus, hinc matrona Iuno et
        numquam umeris positurus arcum,   60

qui rore puro Castaliae lavit
crinis solutos, qui Lyciae tenet
    dumeta natalemque silvam,
        Delius et Patareus Apollo.

vis consili expers mole ruit sua: 65
vim temperatam di quoque provehunt
    in maius; idem odere viris
        omne nefas animo moventis.

testis mearum centimanus Gyges
sententiarum, notus et integrae   70
    temptator Orion Dianae,
        virginea domitus sagitta.

iniecta monstris Terra dolet suis
maeretque partus fulmine luridum
    missos ad Orcum, nec peredit   75
        impositam celer ignis Aetnen,

incontinentis nec Tityi iecur
reliquit ales, nequitiae additus
    custos; amatorem trecentae
        Pirithoum cohibent catenae.   80

'Descend from heaven and, come, play upon your pipe, queen
Calliope, a long tune, or if now you prefer, (sing) with your clear
voice or to the strings and lyre of Phoebus (4).

'Are you (all) listening? Or does a delightful feeling of inspiration delude me? I seem to hear you and to stray through holy groves, past which flow pleasant streams and breezes.

'On Apulian Voltur, beyond the limits set by my nurse Pullia (10), when I was a boy, tired with play and sleepiness, the fabled doves concealed me with fresh leaves, so that it was a miracle to all who dwell in the nest of lofty Aceruntia and the glades of Bantia and the rich earth of low-lying Forentum (16), how I slept with my body safe from black vipers and bears and was covered with sacred laurel and myrtle collected together, a spirited infant, not without divine protection (20).

'Under your protection, Muses, under your protection, I climb into the steep Sabine hills, or if chill Praeneste or Tibur reclining on its hill or cloudless Baiae has taken my fancy. Since I was a friend to your fountains and dances (25), neither the battle-line beaten back at Philippi nor the accursed tree nor cape Palinurus in Sicilian waters snuffed me out. So long as you are with me, gladly as a sailor shall I attempt the raging Bosporus (30) and as a wayfarer the burning sands of the Assyrian shore; I shall visit the Britons savage to strangers and the Concanian rejoicing in horses' blood, I shall visit the quivered Geloni (35) and the Scythian river, unscathed.

'You refresh great Caesar in a Pierian cave, as soon as he has disbanded his soldiery, wearied with warfare, among the townships, when he is looking for an end to his labours (40); you both give him gentle counsel and rejoice in its giving, kindly ones.

'We know how he destroyed the impious Titans and their dreadful crew with his crashing thunderbolt, who governs the inert earth, the windy sea (45) and cities and the sad kingdoms (of the dead) and gods and the troops of mortal men, he alone, with his impartial rule.

'Great terror that band of youth had inspired in Juppiter, trusting in its forest of hands (50), and those brothers who strove to set Pelion upon shady Olympus. But what could Typhoeus and strong Mimas or Porphyrion of menacing stature, what could Rhoetus and Enceladus the bold spearman with torn-up trees (56), what could they do hurling themselves against the thundering aegis of Pallas? On this hand stood greedy Vulcan, on that the matron Juno and, never destined to take the bow from his shoulders (60), he who washes his flowing hair in the dew of Castalia, who dwells in the thickets of Lycia and the wood of his birth, Apollo of Delos and Patara.

'Force that is devoid of judgement crashes under its own weight (65): force that is controlled the gods even promote to greater heights, but they despise violence that meditates in its heart all that is wrong. As a witness to my opinions there is hundred-handed Gyges and Orion, famous as the assailant of the virgin Diana, tamed by the maiden's arrow (72). (Mother) Earth, piled over her own monsters, grieves and mourns for her children shot down by the thunderbolt to ghostly Orcus (75), nor has the swift fire eaten through Aetna set on top of it, nor has the bird abandoned the liver of lustful Tityos, set as guardian over his wickedness: three hundred chains confine the lover Pirithous.'

The poem opens with the poet praying to the Muse, Calliope; he addresses her as *regina* for Hesiod called her the noblest of the Muses,[1] and asks her to come down, like the goddess she is, from heaven and play on the pipe (suggesting a choral lyric) or sing or play on the lyre (suggesting a monody like Horace's *Odes*).[2] The prayer ends with the first stanza, there is a pause, then the poet addresses a number of people, asking 'Do you hear?' Commentators take this to mean that the poet addresses his audience (of boys and girls—Ode 1. 4), but such an audience is not addressed elsewhere and it is hard to explain why the poet should turn to such irrelevant people when he is hoping to enjoy the personal experience of inspiration. Later in the poem the Muses are treated as the plurality they were (21 ff., 37 ff., 41 ff.), and it seems more likely that the poet addresses the Muses first in the person of Calliope;[3] then, his prayer completed, he asks hopefully 'are you listening to me?' He follows this by stating the unwelcome alternative; for if the Muses are not listening (and answering), then the pleasant sensation of inspiration (a form of madness, so called *insania*)[4] is deceiving him (*ludit*). He then goes on with increasing confidence: he seems to hear them and to

---

[1] *Theogony* 79 ἣ δὴ προφερεστάτη ἐστὶν ἁπασῶν. There were nine Muses, but it was long after Horace's time that each was assigned a particular branch of literature; he consequently addresses any Muse whom he wishes or all of them together.

[2] For Horace's poetic pretence that he sings his poetry to the lyre, see p. 8 above. Here, the various possibilities suggested to Calliope have a special function since, in fact, this ode, unlike most (which are based on the monodic lyric of Sappho and Alcaeus), is based on a great choral lyric ode of Pindar.

[3] See n. 1 above. Virgil does something of the same sort when he says in *Aeneid* ix. 525 *vos, o Calliope, precor, adspirate canenti*.

[4] Horace describes this sensation in ode 25, and applies words such as *attonitus* (ode 19. 14). The idea that poets are mad, because possessed by some inexplicable outside influence, goes far back in Greek thought (see E. R. Dodds, *The Greeks and the Irrational*, Berkeley, 1951, ch. 3, 'The Blessings of Madness', especially pp. 80–2).

wander through the conventional landscape of inspiration, containing
streams and groves (called 'holy'—*pii*—because only those who are devoted
to—*pii*—the Muses are admitted). The poet has been clear about his in-
spiration, so there is another pause after 5–8, till he begins on his poem
proper.

The first section (9–20) tells of a series of miracles that happened to the
poet when he was young (they are reminiscent of similar happenings which
were told of many of the great Greek poets). What makes the account
remarkable is the authentic note of autobiography given by the name of his
nurse, Pullia (10), and the perfect evocation of obscure little towns in the
region where the poet was born (the 'nest'—*nidum*—is wonderfully precise
for a little hill-town perched, like an eagle's nest, on the very point of the
hill), their names unknown to history but proudly spoken by the poet.

The next stanza looks back over 9–20, and forward to the next section.
The explanation of the miracles is that the poet is protected by the Muses,
but he says this in a way that contrives to mention the regions he loves as a
grown man: the Sabine hill-country and the seaside resort of Baiae; so the
stanza also suggests the poet as an older man. This leads to the more concrete
miracles of his later years (25–8): Philippi, the tree,[1] and drowning off
Sicily (otherwise unknown). The tone has grown more serious, and now (29–
36) the poet seems to review casually in his own mind dangerous parts of
the world, where, yet, the Muses would protect him; but the places happen
to be the great trouble-spots on the borders of the empire—the Black
Sea (30), the Persian Gulf (31–2), Britain (33), Spain (34), and south Russia
(35–6), where the Scythians and Geloni live.

These are names that ring through Roman history, and, so, by a subtle
transition, the poet moves to the picture of Caesar paying off his veteran
troops and settling them in country districts: no doubt the poet is mainly
thinking of 29 B.C. when Octavian returned to celebrate a triple triumph,
and closed the gate of Janus, signifying peace in all the regions reviewed
by Horace in the previous two stanzas. The second strand in the connection
of thought enters here: the Muses look after Caesar too (40),[2] and, in
particular, both give him gentle counsel[3] (i.e. advice to act with clemency)
and are glad to have given it (i.e. because he takes the advice).

But, once again, as the outlines of a real political situation begin to appear,

[1] For the poet's escape from death by a falling tree, see ode 8; for Philippi, see p. 4
above.
[2] The implication here is that Augustus takes an interest in poetry—a fact of which
Horace and Virgil (and others) were well aware: see pp. 6 ff. above.
[3] Line 41 scans *vōs lēnĕ cōnsīli(um) ĕt dătīs ĕt dătō* with the second -*i*- of *consilium*
treated (quite artificially) as consonantal: see also p. 63 below, n. 1.

the poet sheers off,[1] this time into a parable about the battle of the Giants against Juppiter. The treatment of this is developed in three movements.

First, the poet gives a general account of the struggle (42–8) in the form of a contrast between the barbarous impiety of the Titans (42–4) and the ruler of the universe (45–8), the latter described in a hymnic invocation (giving the sense of a poetic laudation of Juppiter) which covers land, sea, cities, underworld, gods, and men—a series which is itself arranged as a succession of contrasting pairs.

Then the poet begins again (49–64) with a different approach to the threat represented by the Giants. It is a nice touch that the great description of Juppiter's strength is followed immediately by the statement of his terror at these terrible creatures[2] (there is horrific emphasis on 50 *bracchiis* because some of the Giants had a hundred hands and the poet generalizes this feature to all of them). This is followed by a review of forces on both sides, arranged to express the horror of the Giants at its worst and then the calm strength of the Olympians which made victory inevitable. This section reaches a climax with a hymnic invocation of Apollo (61–64)[3], parallel to that of Juppiter (45–8).

Now the poet expresses the underlying principle, which he presents as a universal law (65–8) that brute force, devoid of judgement, produces its own destruction. The poem ends with illustrations of this law, which is now expressed as the poet's own view (*mearum . . . sententiarum*),[4] none of them necessarily connected with the battle of the Giants: the crime and fate of Gyges is unknown, but Horace mentions him as laid low, in *Odes* ii. 17. 14. Orion (*temptator* means 'assailant' in a sexual sense and appears here for the first time in Latin, modelled on Greek πειραστής) was killed by Diana, but, like Gyges, he was a Giant (i.e. γηγενής, 'born of Earth'). The poet pictures the misery of Earth over her dead children, but expresses it in such a way that the idea uppermost is burial of the dead (*iniectio terrae—iniecta . . . terra*), not the miraculous imprisonment under Etna or other mountains; the poet finds a quite natural way, too, to speak of Etna, with no miracles implied (75–6).[5] The final pair of examples are of Tityos and Pirithous; the former (punished by having a vulture sitting on him eating out his

---

[1] See p. 42 above.

[2] It is worth emphasizing this point, because most commentators, influenced by the Christian concept of an omnipotent God, think the poet blundered into a tasteless contradiction. Greek and Roman concepts of deity were deeply anthropomorphic.

[3] Almost literally translated from Pindar: see Appendix, no. 3.

[4] On the downright factual tone of the word *sententiarum*, see *Style* C III.

[5] This tendency to rationalize the merely miraculous and legendary into more concrete concepts is characteristic of Horace: see p. 44 above and 141 below.

liver—a relevant part since emotions were thought to be seated in the liver
and the vulture therefore is 'added to him as a guard over his lustfulness')
is connected with what precedes by *nec*, for he too was a Giant, who also
assailed Diana (or her mother Leto). But the final example is added in
asyndeton (with rhyme between the two lines (79–80));[1] for Pirithous was
no Giant, but the king of the Lapiths, an attractive character who went
with Theseus to capture Proserpina from the Underworld and was caught
(cf. *Odes* iv. 7. 27–8 where again he closes the poem). It is a perfect *diminu-
endo* to close the poem and a venial sinner, unlike the horrific Giants.

The clue to the understanding of this complex ode lies in its relationship
to one of Pindar's greatest victory-odes, *Pythian* i. There, the first triad is
an invocation of music (Pindar's poetry was intended to be sung) as the
epitome of harmony, loved by the friends of Zeus but hated by his enemies
(like the giant Typhos, imprisoned under Aetna).[2] A transition is made to the
fame of Hieron of Syracuse and his victory in the chariot-race of 470 B.C.,
then to his great victories over the Etruscans and Carthaginians, and to the
foundation of the new city of Aetna: these themes fill the second, third, and
fourth triads. The ode ends with reflections on responsible and harmonious
kingship. When Horace used this poem as a model for his ode, he had a
number of important problems to deal with. First, while Pindar could talk
of music as the principle of harmony and it was relevant to his own poetic
composition, this was not possible for Horace.[3] Secondly, Pindar was writing
choral lyric on a grand scale, but Horace's poetry was personal lyric and as
such it sprang from the life and emotions of the poet. Horace found a
brilliant solution to both problems at the same time: for music he
substituted poetic inspiration. So he commences with a great prayer for in-
spiration—a prayer which is answered (5–8). What follows—trivial auto-
biographical details and even the name of his nurse—often gives offence to
commentators, but this is to miss the point. This section of the poem cor-
responds to Pindar's exposition of the power of music, but, in keeping with
the form of personal lyric, Horace illustrates the power of poetic inspiration
from his own life, but the tone becomes progressively more serious and the
examples both more important and more impersonal till the poet comes to
the review of imperial trouble-spots (29–36). A further problem which
Horace met was due to the fact that music and harmony are ideas that
belong together and easily provide an analogy for the political field, and
also that Pindar could make quite plain the relationship between the battle
of the Giants and Hieron's victories for they were extremely creditable.

[1] On this stylistic structure and its analogues, see *Style* B II.
[2] See Appendix, no. 2, for an extract.   [3] See p. 50, n. 2 above.

Not only, however, was Horace disinclined to present a political situation factually in his poetry,[1] but the fact of opposition to Augustus was a topic to be handled with delicacy, and it was not easy to use the concept of poetic inspiration analogously to that of harmony. What Horace has done has been to expound the power of poetic inspiration autobiographically and then treat it as influencing Augustus also—and influencing him in the direction of clemency (41-2). Then as the outlines of a real political situation begin to appear, the poet swerves away into the mythological parable of the Giants battling against the Olympians. The function of this motif is to give the strongest possible warning against opposition to Augustus: this will lead simply to force and destruction.

The elaborate invocation of the Muse with which the poem opens and the representation of the poet as inspired (5-8) have something of the effect of the protest to the Muse at the end of ode 3. The poet may then be forgiven the fabrication of miracles about himself (which the tone also excuses), and the treatment of the myth about the Giants and especially the punishments of violence (69-80) as if they were factual are excused not only in virtue of their functioning as parables or examples but also because they come as direct inspiration from the Muses.

5

Caelo tonantem credidimus Iovem
regnare: praesens divus habebitur
    Augustus adiectis Britannis
       imperio gravibusque Persis.

milesne Crassi coniuge barbara   5
turpis maritus vixit et hostium—
    pro curia inversique mores!—
       consenuit socerorum in armis,

sub rege Medo Marsus et Apulus,
anciliorum et nominis et togae   10
    oblitus aeternaeque Vestae,
       incolumi Iove et urbe Roma?

[1] See p. 37, n. 2 above.

hoc caverat mens provida Reguli
dissentientis condicionibus
    foedis et exemplo trahenti[1]   15
        perniciem veniens in aevum,

si non periret immiserabilis
captiva pubes: 'signa ego Punicis
    adfixa delubris et arma
        militibus sine caede' dixit   20

'derepta vidi; vidi ego civium
retorta tergo bracchia libero
    portasque non clausas et arva
        Marte coli populata nostro.

auro repensus scilicet acrior   25
miles redibit. flagitio additis
    damnum: neque amissos colores
        lana refert medicata fuco,

nec vera virtus, cum semel excidit,
curat reponi deterioribus.   30
    si pugnat extricata densis
        cerva plagis, erit ille fortis

qui perfidis se credidit hostibus,
et Marte Poenos proteret altero,
    qui lora restrictis lacertis   35
        sensit iners timuitque mortem.

hic, unde vitam sumeret inscius,
pacem duello miscuit. o pudor!
    o magna Carthago, probrosis
        altior Italiae ruinis!'   40

---

[1] All manuscripts give *trahentis*, but this makes Regulus 'deduce from the precedent destruction on the coming age' which is heavily didactic. More poetic is the idea that the precedent itself was bringing destruction on future ages, so *trahenti* is printed though it is doubtful whether any ancient authority exists for it.

fertur pudicae coniugis osculum
parvosque natos ut capitis minor
  ab se removisse et virilem
    torvus humi posuisse vultum,

donec labantis consilio patres   45
firmaret auctor numquam alias dato,
  interque maerentis amicos
    egregius properaret exsul.

atqui sciebat quae sibi barbarus
tortor pararet; non aliter tamen   50
  dimovit obstantis propinquos
    et populum reditus morantem

quam si clientum longa negotia
diiudicata lite relinqueret,
  tendens Venafranos in agros   55
    aut Lacedaemonium Tarentum.

'We have always believed that Juppiter the Thunderer reigns in heaven: Augustus will be held a god present to help us on earth when the Britons and the dangerous Persians have been included in the empire (4).

'Has the soldier of Crassus lived on, a husband disgraced by a barbarian wife, and—alas, the change in government and character!—has he grown old in the service of his fathers-in-law, a Marsian or Apulian under a Persian king, forgetful of the shields and the name and the toga (10) and eternal Vesta, while Juppiter stands safe and the city of Rome?

'This the prophetic mind of Regulus had foreseen when he advised against the disgraceful terms and a precedent (15) that, were the young men in captivity not left to die without pity, promised destruction for future ages: "I have seen the standards of our legions nailed up in Carthaginian temples and weapons taken from our soldiers without bloodshed", he said (20); "I have seen the arms of freeborn Roman citizens tied behind their backs and city-gates open and fields that our army had devastated being cultivated again.

Ransomed with money, I suppose the soldier will return all the keener for battle (26)! You simply compound disgrace with financial loss. Stained with dye, wool gives no sign of its lost colour; and real courage, once it has been lost, refuses to be replaced in the degenerate (30). Only if the deer fights after it has been released from dense nets will he be brave who has given himself up to a perfidious enemy and only then will he crush the Carthaginians in a further war who has felt the thongs tighten on his pinioned wrists (35) and, fearing death, has yet done nothing about it. Such a man, not realizing how to win his life, has just confused peace with war. O honour lost! O great Carthage, greater still by the shameful fall of Italy!" (40).

'They say that he refused the kiss of his chaste wife and his little sons as one who had forfeited his citizenship, and that he set his brave gaze stubbornly on the ground, until he could steady the wavering senators (45) with such advice as was never given before or since, and could then hurry away from among his weeping friends, a distinguished exile. And yet he knew what the barbarous torturer had waiting for him (50): but he moved aside the relatives who stood in his path and the people who would delay his return, just as if a client's lengthy case were finished and the verdict given and he were setting off for the country round Venafrum (55) or for Lacedaemonian Tarentum.'

The poem opens with a generalization, apparently directed elsewhere which nevertheless contains within it the subject of the ode: this amounts to saying that as Juppiter the Thunderer[1] has always been held a god in heaven, so Augustus will be held a god, present to help on earth,[2] when he has conquered Britain and Parthia. The next two stanzas (5-12) vividly turn the readers eyes to a shocking sight: Roman prisoners, survivors from the destruction of Crassus' legions in 53 B.C., fine Italians from Marsia and Apulia, living with Parthian wives and fighting on the side of their fathers-in-law, forgetful of their own national life—the shields (sacred objects kept

---

[1] Augustus dedicated a temple to Iuppiter Tonans on the Capital in gratitude for escape from death by lightning when he was on the Spanish campaign (Suetonius *Aug.* 29. 1 ff., 91. 2). But worship of Iuppiter in this form was, no doubt, ancient (see p. 36 above, n. 2).

[2] Horace never speaks of Augustus as a god on earth, but either associates him with gods (as in ode 3. 9 ff.: see p. 42 above) or speaks of his rule on earth as analogous to that of Juppiter in heaven (see *Odes* i. 12. 49-60). The concept here is a form of this latter idea.

by the Salii), the name of Rome, the national dress, the eternal flame of Vesta (symbol of the empire). This list is completed by an adaptation of an ancient and solemn formula:[1] *salva urbe atque arce*, a phrase signifying the safety of the city of Rome and of the Capitol where was the temple of Juppiter Optimus Maximus, the national god of the Roman state. These two stanzas are alive with patriotism and indignation, but not primarily at the wretched prisoners: it is the Senate and changed character of the Roman people that are to blame who have allowed the wretched prisoners to live for a quarter of a century or more and done nothing about them. This connects these stanzas to the opening generalization: the implication is that Rome must conquer Parthia.

Now the poet's mind goes back more than two centuries to an event in Roman history that had been built up into a legend and been made largely unhistorical in the process. M. Atilius Regulus was captured with five hundred men by the Carthaginians in 255 B.C. and was sent on parole to Rome to negotiate[2] peace or, at least, exchange of prisoners: he advised against either course and returned to face death. Horace has given entirely new life to the old legend by concentrating on a few significant minutes when Regulus made his speech to the Senate and then left his relatives and friends. The speech (18–40) is simple and powerful. Regulus has seen Roman standards in Carthaginian temples (as Horace's contemporaries knew there were Roman standards in Parthian temples) and Roman soldiers allowing themselves to be captured (18–22); even worse, the gates of Carthage are open and they are tilling their fields (confident that Rome will not attack). Sarcasm breaks through in *scilicet*: 'I suppose a ransomed soldier will be all the keener to fight' (25–6). It is not only disgraceful but also a waste of money to buy back men who have allowed themselves to be captured (26–36): such men do not understand the conditions of war—you cannot save your life by cowardice (37–8). The speech ends by echoing the sentiment of the poet as he contemplated Roman inaction against Parthia (7).

Having spoken, Regulus kept his eyes on the ground, refusing to kiss wife or children since he was a slave through capture by the enemy;[3] he

---

[1] The formula can be traced in ancient oaths and perhaps was also an element in the triumphing general's hymn: see G. Williams, *Tradition and Originality in Roman Poetry*, 366 ff.

[2] On the tone of *condicionibus*, see *Style* C III.

[3] A man captured in war automatically became the slave of his captors and thereby lost all rights as a free citizen. The word *caput* expresses a man's personality as free citizen with specific rights, and the technical phrase for the loss of such rights was *deminutio capitis*. The poet naturally avoids technical language; so he speaks of the man as *minor* ('diminished') and limits this by adding *capitis* where the genitive case functions as a genitive of reference ('in respect of his citizen rights').

waited long enough to ensure that the senate came to the right decision and then went off, a distinguished exile. The poet, however, retraces that departure, which he has just related from Regulus' point of view, in order to look at it from the neutral observer's. The analogy with the lawyer going for a well-earned vacation to an estate in the country or the beautiful watering-place of Tarentum is a memorable ending to a straightforward poem that expresses something more than a simple patriotism.

Horace finds an ingenious way in this poem of letting a real political situation appear in outline. He had used elsewhere the idea, which had been used by Greek poets before him, of describing the greatness of Augustus' rule by making it the analogy on earth of Juppiter's in heaven (e.g. *Odes* i. 12. 49–60). Here he modifies that analogy to promise Augustus men's respect as for a divinity on earth after Britain and Parthia have been added to the empire. It seems that Rome had plans, early in Augustus' principate, of following up the abortive landings that Julius Caesar had made in Britain in 55/4 B.C., but this was never done. Horace couples his allusion to this with a design which was in the forefront of Roman thinking throughout the twenties. The disaster at Carrhae in 53 B.C. had been followed by further defeats for Rome on the eastern border, and a consolidation of that region was essential to the stability of the empire. In the end a peace-treaty was made with Parthia in 20 B.C. (with return of the legionary standards captured in 53 B.C.) and this was represented as a victory. The political situation which Horace faintly allows to appear is that of military planning against Britain and Parthia. The mention of the former is something of a poetic red-herring[1] and the poet instantly sheers off to a most unexpected portrait of a forgotten band of men. But he depicts them in no concrete way that might have immediate connection with the political situation in Rome; they are presented in terms of their own outlook, forgotten and forgetting. What the poet evokes is not primarily indignation at their behaviour, but the shame of Romans for a convenient lapse of memory; this is done in an allusive way that has nothing of the preacher about it and the poet instantly leaves the topic for the portrait of Regulus which comes as a nicely calculated surprise.

This was quite a hackneyed legend, but the poet brings it alive with a completely new treatment. He concentrates on a few hours in Regulus' life, but, in the speech, he conveys all that has gone before, with an excellent picture of Carthage as seen from a prisoner's point of view; this speech moves through a series of tones from indignation to sarcasm to shame. Then, where there was danger of a sentimental treatment, the poet quotes a contemporary eye-witness's report (41–8). Finally, with a strongly

[1] See p. 42 above.

contrasting particle *atqui*[1] he views the same scene by means of an analogy, from his objective poet's point of view, taken from the very centre of normal life at Rome. It is a sharply devised contrast to the grim reality.

6

Delicta maiorum immeritus lues,
Romane, donec templa refeceris
   aedesque labentis deorum et
      foeda nigro simulacra fumo.

dis te minorem quod geris, imperas: 5
hinc omne principium, huc refer exitum;
   di multa neglecti dederunt
      Hesperiae mala luctuosae.

iam bis Monaeses et Pacori manus
inauspicatos[2] contudit impetus   10
   nostros et adiecisse praedam
      torquibus exiguis renidet;

paene occupatam seditionibus
delevit urbem Dacus et Aethiops,
   hic classe formidatus, ille   15
      missilibus melior sagittis.

fecunda culpae saecula nuptias
primum inquinavere et genus et domos;
   hoc fonte derivata clades
      in patriam populumque fluxit: 20

---

[1] On the change of tone introduced by this word, see *Style* C III.

[2] One half of the manuscript tradition gives *inauspicatos* and this is preferable to *non auspicatos* of the other half since Horace liked the use of the privative prefix *in-*. Many such formations appear in him for the first time in Latin, e.g. *iniussus*, *inaudax*, *inominatus*, *inaratus*, *inputatus*, etc. The short syllable at the beginning of the line is no objection: it occurs two dozen times in the first three lines of Alcaic stanzas outside these examples from *Odes* iii—1. 2 and 26; 3. 34 and 71; 4. 78; 5. 22.

motus doceri gaudet Ionicos
matura virgo et fingitur artibus
    iam nunc et incestos amores
        de tenero meditatur ungui;

mox iuniores quaerit adulteros   25
inter mariti vina, neque eligit
    cui donet impermissa raptim
        gaudia luminibus remotis,

sed iussa coram non sine conscio
surgit marito, seu vocat institor   30
    seu navis Hispanae magister,
        dedecorum pretiosus emptor.

non his iuventus orta parentibus
infecit aequor sanguine Punico,
    Pyrrhumque et ingentem cecidit   35
        Antiochum Hannibalemque dirum,

sed rusticorum mascula militum
proles, Sabellis docta ligonibus
    versare glaebas et severae
        matris ad arbitrium recisos   40

portare fustis, sol ubi montium
mutaret umbras et iuga demeret
    bobus fatigatis, amicum
        tempus agens abeunte curru.

damnosa quid non imminuit dies?   45
aetas parentum peior avis tulit
    nos nequiores, mox daturos
        progeniem vitiosiorem.

'You will expiate the sins of your ancestors, though you do not
deserve to, citizen of Rome, until you have rebuilt the temples and

the ruined shrines of the gods and the images fouled with black smoke. You hold sway because you keep yourself subject to the gods (5): from this should come every beginning, to this refer each end; neglected, the gods have brought many disasters on grieving Italy: twice already, Monaeses and the band of Pacorus have crushed attacks by us that had no divine auspices (10), and they grin with joy to have added spoils from us to their meagre ornaments; the Dacian and the Ethiopian almost destroyed our city, preoccupied with its seditions—the latter formidable with his fleet (15), the former more skilled with missile arrows.

'Generations prolific in sin first polluted marriage and the family and home; ruin, channelled from this source, flowed out over country and people (20): the girl, come of age, delights to learn Ionic dances and is trained in the arts of entertainment and even now thinks upon illicit love with all her young heart; soon, at parties with her husband, she seeks younger adulterers (25) and she does not (trouble to) choose the man to whom she may give forbidden pleasures—neither hurriedly, nor with the candles removed; for, asked quite openly, she gets up, with her husband's full knowledge, whether the request comes from a travelling salesman (30) or the master of a Spanish ship, an expensive purchaser of her disgrace.

'Not from parents like this did the youth arise which stained the sea with the blood of Carthage and slew Pyrrhus and great (35) Antiochus and terrible Hannibal, but a masculine race born of rustic warriors, skilled to turn the turves with Sabine spades and, at the bidding of an upright mother, to bring home cut (40) wood when the sun was altering the shadows of the mountains and was taking the yokes from weary oxen, bringing with his flying chariot the friendly time of night.

'What has destructive time not diminished (45)? The age of our parents, worse than that of our grandparents, has produced us more wicked still, soon to give birth to a progeny yet more degenerate.'

The poem opens with a general warning to Roman citizens: the present generation is not guilty, but their ancestors allowed the temples of the gods to fall into disrepair; these must be rebuilt if the penalty for the sins of their fathers is to be avoided. There is a historical background to this warning. In his sixth consulship (28 B.C.), Augustus inaugurated a programme of rebuilding the temples; he was proud of this and records (*res gestae* 20. 4) that he rebuilt eighty-two temples of the gods in Rome. The general theory on which the warning is based is now stated (5–6): the Romans hold their empire because they are god-fearing—this is the principle from which every-thing should begin (*hinc omne principium*[1]—the reader is to understand *pete* out of *refer*) and with which everything should end. By the time Horace was writing it was almost a commonplace explanation (among others) of Roman military success: the natural piety of Romans made them superior to other races.[2] In expressing this generalization the poet has given the ground for his warning (1–4), but he now gives support for the generaliza-tion itself by looking at the very recent past of his own generation (11 *nostros*). The record is grim: shameful defeats on the eastern border suffered by L. Decidius Saxa in 40 B.C. at the hands of Pacorus and by Oppius Statianus in 36 B.C. at the hands of Monaeses (Antony was the general commander of the Roman forces); then, more recently, there was the near-defeat of Actium (regarded here by the poet as a battle with Egypt) and the related incursion of the Dacians on the Rumanian border. This is an impressive passage, sombre with telling details (like the savage grins of the Parthians over the Roman dead) and echoing with great names from recent history. It is an interesting treatment that makes Actium not a battle in the civil war (which it was) but a battle against the Egyptians (loosely called Aethiopians) that the Romans almost lost through the distraction of civil war. This was the official view and Octavian actually celebrated a triumph for it. The result is to represent Actium as a battle which the true forces of Rome were almost made to lose through Roman civil war, and so to put the blame on the previous generation in such a way that Actium becomes a success won in spite of them. The tone of this section of the poem (1–16) is optimistic: the evil events (9–16) are expressed in past tenses, and Romans do hold their empire (5 *imperas*) and they are repairing the temples (1–4).

There is a pause, and a general statement totally pessimistic in tone comes as a surprise (17–18), both for its tone and also because the poet's vision has moved far further back into the past (17 *saecula*). His view now takes in a different aspect of Roman life—that of the family and the home and marriage; these institutions have been stained by sin and this has been the source of the disaster which flowed out over the people and state. There follows one of those sudden pictures which Horace catches so vividly: here that of a young girl, corrupted from her earliest years (*motus Ionicos* were dances regarded as indecent) so that she throws herself wholeheartedly (this is the meaning of *de tenero ungui*)[3] into plans for unchastity (*incestos amores*—not incest).

---

[1] Line 6 scans *hinc ŏmnĕ principi(um)*, *hūc rĕfĕr ĕxĭtŭm*, with the third -*i*- of *principium* treated artificially as consonantal (see p. 51 above, n. 3).

[2] See p. 44 above, n. 1.

[3] See, in detail, pp. 66–7 below.

Then she is no sooner married than she is looking for adulterers younger than her husband (*iuniores*) at drinking-parties (*inter mariti vina*). But her husband is not drunk: he connives for profit (32 *pretiosus*) at her adultery. She does not even bother to choose her men[1] (26–7) and they equally are quite prepared to ask her to her face (29)—instead of sending a messenger or letter; the men are vulgar, not even Roman, but rich—travelling salesmen or a Spanish ship's captain.[2] On that note the portrait of the girl ends, and all the tenses have been present, indicating that the poet is analysing his own contemporary society.

But now, with a sharply contrasting *non his . . .* , the poet's vision turns right back to a far past, two or three centuries earlier, to the great period of Roman conquest and expansion in the third and second centuries B.C.— the defeat of Pyrrhus in 275 B.C., of Hannibal in 202 B.C. and of Antiochus in 190 B.C., all hard-won wars of the greatest significance, involving the Romans in abandoning the land and taking to the sea (34). Three stanzas (33–44), corresponding to the three about the girl (21–32), create a completely different portrait of a youth reared in hardship in a farming community up in the Sabine hills, far from the centres of urban corruption;[3] they are sons of soldiers (37) who are away at the wars—hence the emphasis on the mother. Their work was hard but the poet catches the sense of an ideal life unforgettably in a picture of evening coming on, the time of rest, and the shadows lengthening over Italian hills. It is a deeply felt and deeply patriotic picture to complete the poet's evocation of his country's great past. But it is the past, and the poem ends on a note of despair, perfectly expressed to make increasing degeneration span four generations, including the poet's own. The future now looks even darker than the past.

There seems to be a contradiction in this poem between the tones of its two parts (1–16, 17–48): the former optimistic, the latter deeply pessimistic. The contradiction can be epitomized by contrasting (1) *immeritus* with the last stanza (45–8), for the generation described as *immeritus* comes late in the

---

[1] The idea here is not that respectable women in such situations would choose their men, but that she is doubly depraved in her lack of interest in the men as individuals; she is not only promiscuous but also quite indiscriminate. The poet's point can be illustrated by contrast with Catullus' Lesbia, who could at least not be accused of failing to exercise a strong personal preference in the selection of her lovers. Horace's girl is also shameless since she does not feel it necessary to act hurriedly and furtively (*raptim*) or to have the lights removed.

[2] The party at which the poet imagines all this happening is a drinking-party such as that described in ode 19; such parties naturally ended with love-making— here, however, the partner is no flute-girl but a Roman matron, and her husband profits from her disgrace.

[3] This concept is related to the moral ideal of poverty: see p. 34 above, n. 1.

statement of progressive decline. The poem opens with the poet, as so often, just allowing the outline of a political situation to appear;[1] here it is the programme of rebuilding temples inaugurated by Augustus in 28 B.C. But the poet moves instantly away to the concept which underlies Roman worship of the gods: the idea that respect for the gods makes Rome an imperial nation. Is there a political situation underlying the second section of the poem? Three features not only show clearly that there is but also make its identity unmistakable: (i) the final pessimism, to which the poet can set no limit, suggests the failure of all attempts to remedy the evil; (ii) the nature of the evil is stated specifically (17–18) as being sin disruptive of the home and marriage-bond; (iii) the faults of the girl are that she is married and commits adultery and that she does this with the connivance of her husband for gain. It can be no coincidence that these crimes of adultery and connivance were a major target of Augustus' moral legislation. In fact, all three features indicate clearly that the failure of that legislation in 28 B.C. lies behind the second section of the poem. The whole poem, therefore, has the year 28 B.C. as its background, and, just as the year contained contradictory elements of failure and success, so too the poem. What causes the contradiction in the poem is the putting of these two political events side by side, the one a cause for rejoicing, the other for despair. If the poet had been a prose-writer he could have said that it was useless to do the one (i.e. rebuild the temples) without the other (moral reform). It is clear, from the fact that Horace sets the period of Roman excellence (33–44) in the time of the Punic Wars and earlier, that he is relying on a historical theory, widespread in Rome (used by Sallust and Livy) and derived ultimately from the Greek Poseidonius, which dated the beginning of Roman degeneracy from the destruction of Carthage in 146 B.C. The theory was deeply pessimistic and the whole of the second section of the poem (17–48) takes its tone from it; but Horace has created a more complex situation by also taking into account the optimistic sign represented by the rebuilding of the temple. He has managed the transition with skill, for, after stating the generalization in an optimistic form (5–6), he has looked at the disasters of the recent past; in recounting these he moves from disasters suffered at the hands of external enemies to disasters which are really the result of civil war (even Actium is represented as a near-disaster). The poet's tone has become progressively more sombre, and so, after a pause, his gaze naturally travels back beyond these disasters to a more deep-seated cause than neglect of the gods (which has, after all, been remedied). The implication of this connection of thought is that the evils of civil war cannot be regarded as a thing of the past so long as the Romans refuse moral

[1] See p. 42 above.

reform;[1] a rebirth of respect for the gods is a good thing, but it does not touch the far more widespread and dangerous cancer in the national life.

The poet never preaches in this poem. The ideas come naturally as a series of pictures in a great vision of contemporary society in its relationship to the past of Rome, both recent and remote. Much is left to the reader and there is the sense of mystery and of things unsaid that belongs to great poetry. It is worth contrasting this poem with 16 or with the second half of 24, both of which—and especially the former—fall too easily into a directly didactic tone.

What is the meaning of (24) de tenero . . . ungui?

The ancient commentator Porphyrio explains that the phrase derives from a Greek proverb ἐξ ἁπαλῶν ὀνύχων which literally means 'since the nails were soft' and signifies 'from early infancy' (a prima infantia). This is the interpretation accepted by most modern commentators.[2] But there is another Greek phrase ἐξ ὀνύχων, literally 'from one's nails', signifying the equivalent of 'to one's fingertips', i.e. 'totally', 'completely', 'with all one's being'. There is no sign that this phrase was common in Greece and the best authority for it is a work doubtfully ascribed to Plutarch (de liberis educandis 5) and an epigram by the late epigrammatist, Rufinus (Anth. Pal. v. 14. 4). In spite of general agreement, the former meaning seems impossible here.

(i) The poet concentrates on the portrait of the teenage girl before (21–4) and after (25 ff.) marriage: even before marriage she anticipates that state notionally and goes beyond it in her plans. To trace her over-ambitious thoughts back to infancy would be both silly and irrelevant.

(ii) If de tenero . . . ungui is given this temporal sense, then (23) iam nunc must be insulated from meditatur. This can only be done by taking iam nunc strictly with et fingitur artibus as the last element of the clause; yet this is difficult since the influence of iam nunc extends over neighbouring clauses,[3] and it is extremely clumsy to treat this adverbial phrase, normally first (or early) in its sentence, as the last element of a clause. It is far more elegant to take et in 23 as postponed; Horace often postpones et to the second position (but not further) in the Odes, and here iam nunc forms an inseparable unity

---

[1] This theme is also an element of ode 24.

[2] Detailed defences can be found by J. C. Rolfe, Trans. Amer. Phil. Ass. 33 (1902), lxii–iii, and by A. Cameron, Class. Quart. N.S. 15 (1965), 80–3.

[3] Bentley defended the defining of nunc out of de tenero ungui by referring to Epist. ii. 1. 127; but there the poet places himself imaginatively in each stage of the child's growth and traces the poet's influence. In Odes iii. 6. 21–4 he defines the stage in the words matura virgo and iam nunc cannot avoid being defined—together with the other two parallel clauses—from that point.

so that *et* is being postponed to the earliest possible position in the clause. If this is true, then the temporal sense of *de tenero . . . ungui* is excluded.

(iii) It is noticeable that Horace has written the singular *ungui* where all Greek and Latin examples of the expression (except one: see below) have the plural. It is hard to think that the poet would have made this alteration if he had intended a temporal sense (for which the plural would be idiomatic).

(iv) He has also written *de* where all other writers put *ab* or *ex*. In a temporal sense *de* has two significances: (*a*) 'immediately after' a point in time (so, e.g., *de cibo ambulare*), and (*b*) 'before the expiry of' a period of time (so, e.g., *de die potare, de tertia vigilia proficisci*, etc.). Neither sense suits Horace, *Odes* iii. 6. 24. On the other hand *de*, as opposed to *ab* or *ex*, exactly represents the force of ἐξ in ἐξ ὀνύχων as opposed to ἐξ in ἐξ ἁπαλῶν ὀνύχων.

All of these considerations combine to suggest that in *de tenero . . . ungui* Horace was working out a novel form of expression which would give force to his concept of the deep physical intensity of the girl's concentration on *incestos amores*: this is underlined by a use of *de* which expresses the idea of extent inwards from an outer limit—here the finger-nails are, as it were, the absolute outer limit of sensation. The addition of *tenero*, perhaps suggested by the common proverbial use of the phrase, here simply has the function of emphasizing the girl's youth (cf. *tener unguis* in Propertius i. 20. 39 and *tenuis unguis* in Catullus 62. 43 and Ovid *Heroides* iv. 30). The novelty of Horace's phrase, combined with the familiarity of the proverbial *a teneris unguibus*, formed a ready trap for commentators, and when Claudian (*VI Cons. Hon.* 79 f.) wrote *tenero conceptus ab ungue* ('conceived in earliest years') he was, no doubt, relying on this misinterpretation of Horace, *Odes* iii. 6. 24, which commentaries on the *Odes* will have fixed by his time.

7

Quid fles, Asterie, quem tibi candidi
primo restituent vere Favonii
 Thyna merce beatum,
  constantis iuvenem fide

Gygen? ille Notis actus ad Oricum   5
post insana Caprae sidera frigidas
 noctes non sine multis
  insomnis lacrimis agit.

atqui sollicitae nuntius hospitae,
suspirare Chloen et miseram tuis   10
   dicens ignibus uri,
      temptat mille vafer modis.

ut Proetum mulier perfida credulum
falsis impulerit criminibus nimis
   casto Bellerophontae   15
      maturare necem refert;

narrat paene datum Pelea Tartaro,
Magnessam Hippolyten dum fugit abstinens;
   et peccare docentis
      fallax historias monet.   20

frustra: nam scopulis surdior Icari
voces audit adhuc integer. at tibi
   ne vicinus Enipeus
      plus iusto placeat cave,

quamvis non alius flectere equum sciens   25
aeque conspicitur gramine Martio,
   nec quisquam citus aeque
      Tusco denatat alveo.

prima nocte domum claude neque in vias
sub cantu querulae despice tibiae,   30
   et te saepe vocanti
      duram difficilis mane.

'Why weep for Gyges, Asterie, a young man of steadfast fidelity
whom cloudless west winds will restore to you at the beginning
of spring rich with merchandise of Bithynia (5)? He, driven in to
Oricus by storms from the South after (the rising of) Capra's wild
star, spends chill nights, sleepless, with many a tear (8).

  'And yet a messenger from his excited hostess, telling him that
Chloe sighs and is desperately in love with your lover, tempts him

cunningly in a thousand ways (12). He recalls how a faithless
woman with false accusations drove the credulous Proetus to bring
an early death on Bellerophon who was too chaste (16); he tells of
Peleus almost sent down to Tartarus through saying 'No' and re-
fusing Hippolyte of Magnesia; and, in an underhand way, he warns
him of stories that teach him to sin (20).

'In vain: for, deafer than the rocks of Icarus, he hears the voices
and is untouched (22).

But take care that your neighbour Enipeus does not find more
favour with you than is right (24)—though no other is seen on the
field of Mars so skilful to control a horse nor does any so speedily
swim down the Tuscan stream (28). At nightfall lock your house and,
at the quavering note of a flute, do not look down into the street
below, and, though he often calls you hard-hearted, stay stubborn.'

The first two stanzas set the situation as the poet ostensibly comforts Asterie:
her lover Gyges, sailing home from Bithynia, was caught by the winter
storm-winds from the south (*Notus*) and driven to take refuge in Oricus,
on the wrong (i.e. Greek) side of the Adriatic, about the middle of September
(when Capella rises early in the sky). He will reach Italy in spring (when
gentle west winds blow and sailing starts again). It is a coherent story: Gyges
is a merchant, trading with the East, and, business being good (*Thyna merce
beatum*), he postponed his home voyage as long as possible—too long, as it
turned out. He now lies awake at night, cold and miserable without Asterie,
to whom he is constant (the archaic form of the genitive *fide* is not only
metrically convenient, it also adds an impressiveness of tone to the assertion
of his constancy).[1]

The word *atqui* (9) denotes a change of tone:[2] the news is potentially
disturbing. His hostess, Chloe, is in love with him and tells him as much in
messages (*tuis . . . ignibus uri* could mean either 'she is afire with the same
flame as you' or more probably since *ignes* can mean 'object of love', 'she
is in love with your lover'). She keeps reminding him of two sinister stories,
in both of which a woman, in love with a house-guest but rejected by him,
made false accusations to her husband in the hope that he would kill the
guest: so Stheneboea tried to get Proetus to kill Bellerophon, and Hippolyte
tried to get Acastus to kill Peleus. The stories add a point for the reader,
not otherwise stated: Chloe is married, and these are threats of similar action.
So these—and other—stories 'advise him to sin' (19-20). The poet has now
reached the climax in his story, and the single word *frustra*, at the beginning

---

[1] See *Style* A I (*b*).   [2] See *Style* C III.

of the next stanza (as in 13. 6), dramatically resolves it. Gyges is deafer than a rock.

But now a surprise turn comes as the poet warns Asterie herself against becoming too interested in her neighbour Enipeus, however good he is at riding over the Campus Martius or swimming in the Tiber. He ends (29–32) with a pleasing picture of a serenade, and advice to her not to listen.

As so often in Horace the world of the poem is an amalgam of things Greek and things Roman. The names of the characters are Greek. Nothing more than that can be said about Asterie; but Gyges carries on trade in eastern Roman provinces just like a Roman merchant; and, even more, Asterie's neighbour is a perfect example of the model Augustan young man, devoted to athletic training and good at it.[1] The poem implies quite a complex situation, involving four people, which the reader is left to construct for himself from unobtrusive clues: this is an effective technique and is handled with great skill by Horace. The poem also changes tone several times as the poet moves through surprising and effectively managed transitions, keeping for a climax the revelation of the girl's temptation—unexpected, because the poet has concentrated the reader on the situation of Gyges, arousing sympathy for Asterie. In this surprise ending the poem shows itself to be an example of the epigram-form elevated and expanded into a major literary form.[2]

8

Martiis caelebs quid agam Kalendis,
quid velint flores et acerra turis
plena miraris positusque carbo in
    caespite vivo,

docte sermones utriusque linguae?   5
voveram dulcis epulas et album
Libero caprum prope funeratus
    arboris ictu.

hic dies anno redeunte festus
corticem adstrictum pice dimovebi.
amphorae fumum bibere institutae
    consule Tullo.

[1] See p. 35 above, n. 2.   [2] See *Style* E III.

sume, Maecenas, cyathos amici
sospitis centum et vigiles lucernas
perfer in lucem: procul omnis esto   15
    clamor et ira.

mitte civilis super urbe curas:
occidit Daci Cotisonis agmen,
Medus infestus sibi luctuosis
    dissidet armis,   20

servit Hispanae vetus hostis orae
Cantaber sera domitus catena,
iam Scythae laxo meditantur arcu
    cedere campis.

neglegens ne qua populus laboret   25
parce privatus nimium cavere et
dona praesentis cape laetus horae:
    linque severa.

'What I a bachelor can be doing on the first of March, what the flowers mean and the box full of incense and the coal set on living turf—are you, filled with the learning of both languages, in perplexity (5)? I had vowed a pleasant feast and a white kid to Bacchus when I was nearly given my funeral by the tree's fall (8). This day, a holiday as a year is completed, shall remove the cork, set in pitch, from a bottle that was put up to drink in the smoke when Tullus was consul (12).

'Drink, Maecenas, a hundred ladles (of wine) to the health of your friend who was saved and prolong the lighted candles till dawn: let all shouting and anger stay far off (16). Put aside political worries about our city: the band of Dacian Cotiso has fallen; the Persian, his own enemy, is in rebellion with weapons that hurt himself (20); the Cantabrian, our ancient enemy on the coast of Spain, is a slave in chains, tamed lately; now the Scythians, with unstrung bows, are planning to retreat from the plains (24). Negligent lest our people anywhere be in trouble, cease, as a private citizen, to be too anxious, and seize happily on the gifts of the present hour: put aside serious matters.'

The poem opens suddenly on a note of astonishment: Maecenas (who is not, however, named till line 13) cannot make out what Horace is up to. He is humorously addressed in an honorific phrase that praises his depth of learning (*sermones* implies treatises, in dialogue-form, on scientific and philosophical topics); but it does not need all that learning to see that Horace, a bachelor, has no business to be solemnly celebrating the 1st of March, the festival of the Matronalia, with flowers and incense and a fire laid on an *ad hoc* altar of turf. The poet kindly explains (6–8) how on that very day, years ago, he had nearly been killed (the word *funeratus* is not known in this sense before Horace and its effect is humorously macabre: 'almost given my funeral by . . .'); he had then vowed sacrifice (of the pleasant sort that gives a meal to the participants no less than to the god) to Bacchus. So, he goes on, this day (meaning 'today') is a festival for him and will see the cork removed from a bottle that was laid down in the consulship of L. Volcacius Tullus in 66 B.C. (the year before the poet's own birth). This stanza strikes a familiar note in Horace, for it institutes preparations for a drinking-party: wine was stored in *amphorae*, earthenware vessels (with the cork set in pitch) which were marked with the year (i.e. by means of the consul's name) and put up in the *apotheca* at the top of the house, where they were exposed to the smoke (which, Romans thought, had a mellowing effect on wine).

The next stanza (13–16) sees the poet issuing a series of orders, and the addressee's name is postponed to this important point. The orders are being given to Maecenas and, since they concern the way in which the party is to be conducted and particularly the drinking of the wine, it can only be that the poet has constituted himself *arbiter bibendi* or master of ceremonies. So he tells Maecenas to drink one hundred ladles (the number signifying an indefinitely large number) to the health of his friend whose life was saved (the genitive *amici . . . sospitis* imitates a Greek manner of speech, for, when a toast was proposed, where we say 'to so-and-so', the Greeks said—quite naturally since the toast in a sense belongs to the person honoured—'of so-and-so'). Then he bids Maecenas keep the candles burning till dawn—for a pleasant party would, of course, continue as long as possible. But the third order—not, like the previous two, directed to Maecenas, but general—is puzzling at first sight;[1] the poet has not mentioned other guests present, so why should he anticipate noise and quarrelling? The answer is that he does not, but drinking-parties were normally apt to degenerate into rowdy affairs, and he simply indicates that this party will not be of that sort. In fact, there is no suggestion that anyone beside Maecenas is present.

---

[1] On the structure of this stanza, see *Style* B II.

The final three stanzas (17–28) are addressed intimately to Maecenas as the poet urges him to put aside political (*civiles*) worries, and then surveys the worst trouble-spots on the borders of the empire; the Dacians in Rumania, the Parthians in the east (happily occupied in civil war), the Cantabrians in Spain and the Scythians in south Russia. None of these ancient foes is in a position to give trouble. Many attempts have been made to date the poem by these references, but Horace's words are usually imprecise on this subject: the references would suit a time about 27 B.C. More important is the fact that they would not suit a time soon after the battle of Actium when Octavian left Maecenas in charge of the city of Rome (he returned in 29 B.C.). Consequently the worries which Horace attributes to Maecenas are not the result of a semi-official position, but the poet flatters Maecenas by suggesting that he is closely involved in the highest affairs of state. The last stanza then begs Maecenas to be 'negligent' (the word is very strong)[1] and to remember that he is a 'private citizen' (i.e. that he holds no office of state): the tone and sense of these words need further consideration.[2]

This is a complex poem. It is noticeable that often in odes which consist of an uneven number of stanzas, Horace has arranged the material so that it is divided into two blocks with a central connecting stanza. That is the case here. The first three stanzas more or less depict preparations for a drinking-party, the central stanza shows the party begun, and the final three show the poet talking to Maecenas in that setting. This arrangement solved a difficulty. The 'philosophy' of drinking-parties is 'eat, drink, and be merry' and 'take no thought for the morrow'; basically it is a self-centred, self-interested view of life, a weak hedonism that only becomes strong when emphasis is put on death and the uncertainty of life. It simply would not do for Horace to urge this view of life on an important man like Maecenas for it would be to debase and ignore the importance of the great political issues in which he participated. What the poet has done in this ode is to create a setting in which it is perfectly appropriate to urge such views on Maecenas after (not before) they have both begun to relax over a bottle of wine. Even so, the poet first surveys the state of the empire in a way that is both poetically effective (for a series of strange, far-off peoples come to life in memorable phrases) and politically serious in a way that gives depth and range to an apparently light-hearted poem. Then the poet jokes with Maecenas, urging him to be 'negligent' and reminding him that he is a private individual, with the implications that he is really neither of these

---

[1] On the tone of this word, see *Style* A 1 (*c*).
[2] On the structure of the stanza as a whole, see *Style* B 11.

things; only after this, and in the same humorous tone, does he urge the hedonistic view of life on Maecenas—and the view is only urged on him 'for the moment', 'for this passing hour' (*praesentis . . . horae*).

This is a poem in which the tone keeps changing and which, above all, requires the reader to construct a complex setting from clues casually dropped in passing. This imaginative demand on the reader is an important element in the poem's originality. But the reader is not required to invent: the poet gives no reason for Maecenas' sudden presence at the beginning of the poem, it is simply to be taken for granted; equally the poet does not mention other guests, so the possibility of their presence plays no part in the poem's setting.

9

Donec gratus eram tibi
nec quisquam potior bracchia candidae
   cervici iuvenis dabat,
Persarum vigui rege beatior.

   'donec non alia magis   5
arsisti neque erat Lydia post Chloen,
   multi Lydia nominis
Romana vigui clarior Ilia.'

   me nunc Thressa Chloe regit,
dulcis docta modos et citharae sciens,   10
   pro qua non metuam mori
si parcent animae fata superstiti.

   'me torret face mutua
Thurini Calais filius Ornyti,
   pro quo bis patiar mori   15
si parcent puero fata superstiti.'

   quid si prisca redit Venus
diductosque iugo cogit aeneo,
   si flava excutitur Chloe
reiectaeque patet ianua Lydiae?   20

'quamquam sidere pulchrior
ille est, tu levior cortice et improbo
iracundior Hadria,
tecum vivere amem, tecum obeam libens.'

'As long as I found favour with you and no young man, preferred
to me, put his arms round your white neck, I flourished richer than
the king of the Persians' (4).

'As long as you were not more deeply on fire for another girl and
Lydia did not take second place to Chloe, I, Lydia of great fame,
flourished more distinguished than Ilia of Rome' (8).

'Now Thracian Chloe rules over me, she who is knowledgeable
in sweet songs and skilled with the lyre, for whom I shall not fear
to die if the fates shall spare my darling to survive me' (12).

'Calais, son of Ornytus of Thurium, burns me with a fire he feels
too, for whom I shall suffer death twice over, if the fates shall
spare the boy to survive me' (16).

'What if our former love returns and forces us, now separated,
together under a brazen yoke, if blonde Chloe is thrown out and the
door opened to Lydia who was rejected?' (20).

'Although he is more beautiful than a star, while you are more
lightweight than a cork and more quick-tempered than the violent
Adriatic, yet with you should I love to live, with you should I
willingly die.'

This is an amoebean song, with verses sung alternately by a man and a girl.
In all amoebean singing there is a competitive element: *Eclogues* 3 and 7
are actual competitions and Catullus 62, where choirs of boys and girls
sing alternately till the boys win, shows the same form. The competitive
element resided in the requirement that the second singer should follow
the form and subject-matter of the first but 'cap' him each time. There is
something of that in this ode.

In this first pair of stanzas the poet contents himself with the modest
statement *donec gratus eram*: 'as long as I found favour with you . . .'. But
Lydia states his passion for other women more strongly with the word
arsisti. Lydia also caps the poet's state of bliss (he was richer than Croesus)
by saying that she was 'of wide renown' (*multi . . . nominis*) and 'more
famous than Roman Ilia'—this was a comparison that would come home
with far more force to Romans since Ilia was the mother of Romulus and
Remus.

The second pair of stanzas contains corresponding confessions of love. The poet will not fear to die for Chloe if the fates spare his darling to survive him (*animae* is a powerful substitute for the lover's phrase *vita mea* 'my life': here the poet calls her 'my soul'—the only element of man eligible to achieve immortality). But again Lydia caps him. Her passion is stronger, for Chloe only 'rules' the poet, while Lydia burns with a love that is returned; also her young man sounds young (16 *puero*) and is far more distinguished than the musically talented Chloe (his name is Greek and his father comes from Thurium, or Sybaris, a place renowned for wealth or luxury). Finally Lydia will suffer death twice for him.

Now the poet asks: 'What if our old love returns and forces us together irresistibly . . .?' Unhesitatingly comes the answer in light-hearted but touching terms that skilfully suggest concealed depths of emotion.

There is no indication of the man's identity, but, in the last stanza, through the girl's words, there just appears the faintest outline of a self-portrait of Horace himself, for fickleness and a quick temper are faults that Horace confesses to in *Satires* ii. 3. 321 ff. and *Epistles* i. 20. 25. It is a very pretty touch that the girl should be allowed this moment of unflattering candour and then make up for it completely in her next words. This candour also has another function. The poem exists in a void, as it were: the reader must understand the setting for himself, but those words of Lydia explain how they came to part, and suggest that the blame lay with the poet. But no ill feeling disturbs the pure calm of the poem: it is a blithe Mozartian duet, ending just at the right point where the reader can sense a deepening of feeling. There is nothing like it in extant Greek poetry: a tiny fragment of a poem of Sappho (121 L.–P.) seems to be from a dialogue between a man and a woman, but nothing is known of its context.

10

Extremum Tanain si biberes, Lyce,
saevo nupta viro, me tamen asperas
porrectum ante foris obicere incolis
    plorares Aquilonibus.

audis quo strepitu ianua, quo nemus   5
inter pulchra satum tecta remugiat
ventis, et positas ut glaciet nives
    puro numine Iuppiter?

ingratam Veneri pone superbiam,
ne currente retro funis eat rota: 10
non te Penelopen difficilem procis
    Tyrrhenus genuit parens.

o quamvis neque te munera nec preces
nec tinctus viola pallor amantium
nec vir Pieria paelice saucius   15
    curvat, supplicibus tuis

parcas, nec rigida mollior aesculo
nec Mauris animum mitior anguibus:
non hoc semper erit liminis aut aquae
    caelestis patiens latus.   20

'If you were a drinker of the so far-off Tanais, Lyce, and married
to a savage husband, yet you would be sorry to expose me, stretched
out before your heartless doors, to the north winds that inhabit the
country (4). Do you hear the noise the door makes, how the clump
of trees, planted amid the pretty buildings, creaks in the gale, and
how Juppiter, with an unclouded divinity, freezes over the lying
snows? (8). Put aside a disdain that is displeasing to Venus, in case the
rope may slip back from the whirling drum: your Etruscan father
did not beget you a Penelope to keep saying 'No 'to suitors (12).
O, although neither gifts nor prayers nor the pallor, tinged with
purple, of your lovers nor your husband desperately in love with a
Pierian mistress move you, spare the lives of those who beg you,
you who are no softer than an unbending oak nor kinder in heart
than Moorish snakes (18): not for ever will this side of mine put up
with your doorstep and the rains from heaven.'

The poet addresses a girl significantly called Lyce (the feminine of the Greek
word for 'wolf') since it will appear that she is, in the poet's view, cruel.
The opening line is a high-flown epic way of saying 'if you lived in south
Russia' (the Tanais is the Don and flows into the Sea of Azov), and the
next phrase adds the further qualification that she should be married to a
Scythian, who would not only be a barbarian but could be expected to act
with uncivilized savagery (*saevo*) against any misconduct on her part. Even
under those conditions, says the poet, she would feel remorse at leaving him

on her doorstep, exposed to the north winds that are the region's inhabitants. The reader is now in possession of the outlines of the situation: the poet is outside Lyce's door, asking for admittance, but she refuses with more cruelty than might be expected of a married woman in Scythia. The poet's tone is reproachful with a solemnity that is mirrored in the elevated language. He now (5–8) calls attention to his immediate surroundings: the wind that makes the door creak and the trees groan, the clear sky (for Juppiter is in origin the Indo-European Sky-God),[1] the heavy frost, and the snow on the ground. This stanza not only describes the weather, but, in the detail of the beautiful house with a grove of trees planted in the courtyard, indicates to the reader the rich luxury of Lyce's house. The poet's tone now changes from reproach to warning (9–12): proud disdain displeases Venus, and Lyce may, in adopting that attitude, have taken on something which she cannot carry through; Venus will find it easy to punish her, for she is no Penelope. Here the metaphor is of a crane used to crank up a heavy weight by winding in a rope on a great wheel-like drum (*rota*): the winder's strength gives out and the weight crashes to the ground. It is excellently unexpected and remote from the topic which it illustrates, yet instantly clear and appropriate. Another detail about Lyce here comes through to the reader: her father was Etruscan, a people proverbially rich, luxurious, and lax in morals, so that she cannot play the part of Odysseus' wife who kept saying 'No' to suitors for twenty years. Again, the poet's tone changes (13 ff.) and becomes plaintive as he recalls his presents to her, his constant pleas, his pale face, drawn with anxiety, and blue with cold. But as he says this, a vicious thought occurs to him, and he reminds her of the unfaithfulness of her husband, deeply in love (*saucius* is a strong word) with his mistress in Macedonia.[2] This is brought in as the last of the considerations which should make her kind to a lover—but this by way of revenge. The poet's anger has been rising as he spoke and, though the next words (*supplicibus tuis parcas*) pick up again the plaintive tone, it is only a brief touch; for he goes straight on to condemn her as harder than oak and no kinder in heart than Mauretanian snakes. From this his tone rises to a threat: he will not always endure lying on her doorstep in the rain.

The poem is a serenade (παρακλαυσίθυρον as the Greeks called it) and a traditional poetic form, handled by many poets, Greek and Roman. Horace has given it a treatment that is quite original, probably because he has regarded himself as taking the form of epigram and upgrading it into

[1] See p. 36 above, n. 2.

[2] The location of the husband in Macedonia is significant. Macedonia had been a Roman province since 146 B.C.; both government and trade would have provided reasons for Romans to be absent there for long periods.

a major poetical form.[1] This has meant that he has left the details of the situation and the characters to be inferred by the reader from clues casually dropped by the poet in a discourse whose purpose is quite different. This is most effective—especially in the gradual revelation of Lyce's life and situation. The changes of tone, too, which are many and dramatic for so short a poem, are excellently managed. Above all, the poet composes in detachment, as it were, so that he achieves an ironic and humorous presentation as he observes himself from outside, allowing himself to appear petulant and ridiculous in a most undignified situation.

11

Mercuri (nam te docilis magistro
movit Amphion lapides canendo)
tuque testudo resonare septem
    callida nervis,

nec loquax olim neque grata, nunc et   5
divitum mensis et amica templis,
dic modos, Lyde quibus obstinatas
    applicet auris,

quae velut latis equa trima campis
ludit exsultim metuitque tangi,   10
nuptiarum expers et adhuc protervo
    cruda marito.

tu potes tigris comitesque silvas
ducere et rivos celeris morari;
cessit immanis tibi blandienti   15
    ianitor aulae

Cerberus, quamvis furiale centum
muniant angues caput eius atque
spiritus taeter saniesque manet
    ore trilingui;   20

[1] See *Style* E iii.

quin et Ixion Tityosque vultu
risit invito, stetit urna paulum
sicca, dum grato Danai puellas
    carmine mulces.

audiat Lyde scelus atque notas   25
virginum poenas et inane lymphae
dolium fundo pereuntis imo,
    seraque fata,

quae manent culpas etiam sub Orco.
impiae—nam quid potuere maius?—   30
impiae sponsos potuere duro
    perdere ferro.

una de multis face nuptiali
digna periurum fuit in parentem
splendide mendax et in omne virgo   35
    nobilis aevum,

'surge,' quae dixit iuveni marito,
'surge, ne longus tibi somnus, unde
non times, detur; socerum et scelestas
    falle sorores,   40

quae velut nactae vitulos leaenae
singulos eheu lacerant: ego illis
mollior nec te feriam neque intra
    claustra tenebo.

me pater saevis oneret catenis,   45
quod viro clemens misero peperci:
me vel extremos Numidarum in agros
    classe releget.

i pedes quo te rapiunt et aurae,
dum favet nox et Venus, i secundo   50
omine et nostri memorem sepulcro
    scalpe querelam.'

'Mercury (for, trained under your teaching, Amphion moved
masonry by singing) and you, tortoise-shell, skilled to resonate to
seven strings (4)—though once you had no voice and were not
popular, yet now you are loved both at the tables of the wealthy
and in temples—teach me a song to which Lyde may apply her
obstinate ears, she who like a three-year-old filly plays skittishly
over the fields and fears to be touched (10), inexperienced in
marriage and unripe yet for a rough husband. You can lead tigers
and woods as your companions, and bring swift rivers to a halt
(14); to you, as you soothed him, the janitor of the vast hall gave
way (16), Cerberus—though a hundred snakes may fortify his
fearful head and foul breath and venom flow from his triple-
tongued mouth (20). Yes, even Ixion and Tityos smiled with un-
willing faces and the urn stood for a time dry as you won the
daughters of Danaus with a delightful song . . . (24).

'Let Lyde hear of the crime and the famous punishment of those
virgins and of the barrel empty of water that flows away at the bot-
tom, and of the late fate (28) that awaits crime even beneath Orcus.

'Wicked women—for what worse could they have done? (30)—
wicked women, they had the heart to murder their betrothed with
pitiless steel. Only one of many, worthy of the marriage-torch, was
magnificently deceitful to her perjured father, a girl famous through
all eternity (36), who said "Get up" to her young husband, "Get up,
lest a long sleep be given you by those you do not fear; escape a
father-in-law and criminal sisters (40) who like lionesses that have
pounced on calves, one by one, alas, tear them to pieces: I, gentler
than they, shall neither stab you nor keep you in prison. Let my
father load me with barbaric chains (45), because, merciful, I
spared my poor husband's life: let him banish me by ship to the
furthest territories of the Numidians. Go whither your feet and the
breezes take you, while night and Venus are on your side: go with
favouring omens and on your tomb carve an epitaph to recall me".'

The ode opens as a prayer in formal style to Mercury and the lyre which
he invented by stretching seven strings across a tortoise-shell. The vocative

Mercuri is followed by a parenthesis introduced by *nam*, explaining why the prayer should be addressed to this particular god. This was a traditional feature of prayers, both Greek and Roman, and it was honorific because it always referred to a feat or power of the god which had helped in the past and would serve on the present occasion too.[1] Here the reference is to Amphion's building of Thebes, for the great stones moved into place of their own accord, to the sound of his music (which Mercury taught him). Then the tortoise-shell receives an honorific address (3–6). Finally, the poet makes his request: it is for a tune suited to Lyde's obstinate ears (7–8), for she is a shy and difficult filly (9–12).

The poet now proceeds to the purely honorific recital of the god's powers and achievements. Normally this would be done with anaphora of *tu*, but here there is only *tu* (13) and *tibi* (15). This is because, though the poet addresses the lyre, he actually concentrates on its achievements in the hands of Orpheus: his leading tigers and woods, his halting swift rivers (13–14), then his descent into the Underworld to bring back Eurydice; but here the poet's interest halts and he concentrates on the well-known inhabitants of the 'vasty hall' (*immanis . . . aulae*), Cerberus, Ixion (on the eternally moving wheel), and Tityos (whose liver was always being eaten out by a vulture), finally the daughters of Danaus. If the stanza 17–20 is genuine,[2] the poet lingers over the horror of Cerberus, a device well calculated to slow the movement and bring the vision to a halt in Hades. It also emphasizes the aggressive frightfulness of Cerberus, from which there is point in going on with the particles *quin et* ('and that is not all but . . .') to an even more surprising fact (for one would have thought that there could be nothing worth mentioning after the retreat of the terrible hound). Yet the next instance is not only more surprising, but also the reverse of the extrovert, aggressive monster, for two men, undergoing horrible tortures, were actually moved to smile (well might the poet add 'with unwilling faces'). Then the poet's thoughts move on to the daughters of Danaus, eternally filling a barrel without a bottom, carrying the water to it in a sieve—a task where, if ever, success depended on swift and dogged continuity: yet they stopped work (22–4). As the poet says these words, it suddenly dawns on him that he has found his subject for Lyde.

In a transitional stanza (25–8) the poet suggests that Lyde should be told of the crime and punishment of the daughters of Danaus, but, as he says this, his thoughts carry him on from the punishment to the enormity of the

[1] In *Aeneid* i. 65 ff. Juno makes a request to Aeolus and Virgil indicates the exaggerated, flattering respect of her address by a parenthetical clause introduced by *namque* immediately after the vocative: *Aeole (namque tibi divom pater atque hominum rex . . .)*. Juno addresses him, as it were, in a prayer.   [2] See pp. 84–5 below.

crime (and so the reader is—deliberately—deprived of knowing just how the poet would have used the story to soften Lyde). Lyde is now forgotten as the poet moves from the crime of the wicked sisters (*impiae* for they lacked wifely dutifulness) to the heroism of Hypermestra who was 'magnificently deceitful' (*splendide mendax*) against her perjured father (who broke his oath to the sons of Aegyptus). The story is told by a favourite device of Horace's, a speech at a significant moment[1]—here it is the moment before Hypermestra bundles her young husband out of her room and down to the harbour (49 *pedes*) where he can take ship (49 *aurae*) to safety (50 *secundo omine*). The poet's picture of her is charming: she uses periphrasis for horrible thoughts: so 'the long sleep' that may be given to him 'whence he does not fear'—she cannot say 'lest I am forced to kill you'. Then her sisters' actions appear in the simile of lionesses, but even so she cannot suppress her horror (42) *singulos eheu lacerant*,[2] and the words (43–4) in which she denies that she will do likewise are very indirect. Her indignation breaks out (45–8) in a pathetic acceptance of her father's vengeance which she anticipates may be either imprisonment or—more emphatically—the purely Roman punishment of banishment (*relegatio*), here by ship (*classe*) and to the savage, dangerous desert regions of Numidia. She then hurries her husband out with good wishes, and a last request for a mention on his tombstone (as, for instance, Turia who saved her husband's life was honoured).[3] When she says 'engrave it', she means, as often in Latin, 'have it engraved'.

The poem is constructed like ode 27 to create a form whereby personal lyric is shaped to accommodate mythological narrative. So the poet starts from an autobiographical premise—Lyde's obstinacy—and he uses this to motivate the prayer and then the prayer to hit—accidentally of course—on the story which he wished to tell. But—as with odes 5 and 27—'story' is the wrong word to use; what the poet does is to take an old story and totally re-cast it by selecting an unexpected point from which to view it: here it is the very dramatic hour of the wedding night when the daughters of Danaus were killing their husbands. The result is a lively and original treatment of a familiar legend.

[1] This technique is to be seen also in odes 3, 5, and 27.

[2] The poet, with gentle irony, plays on his heroine's delicacy of feeling, as he does also (in a different way) in the case of Europa in ode 27. 50 ff. (see p. 139 below).

[3] Turia, wife of Q. Lucretius Vespillo (consul in 19 B.C.), saved her husband's life in the proscriptions of 43/2 B.C. and was honoured by a long *laudatio* which her husband set up over her grave (*CIL* vi. 1527). But the poet could equally well be thinking of an inscription such as Lucius Aurelius Hermia caused to be set up over his own grave and that of his wife who predeceased him (*CIL* i. 2. 1221).

Is the stanza 17–20 interpolated?

There is only one apparently objective argument for regarding the stanza as composed and inserted by a later hand; this is the fact that *eius* is avoided by poets who write the higher genres of poetry (elegiac, epic, and lyric). But this is not a conclusive argument, since the one word might be corrupt, and, in any case, Horace does use *eius* at *Odes* iv. 8. 18; Ovid also uses the word twice in his elegiacs (so too Propertius) and once in his epic *Metamorphoses* (viii. 16). It is certainly true that *eius* followed by *atque* sounds clumsy, but judgement on such a point is difficult to substantiate. Why does Horace write *illius* at *Odes* iv. 13. 18 only, while Ovid uses the word twenty times in his epic? Again, Horace never writes *huius* in the *Odes*, but Ovid does thirty-one times in his epic. Chance and oversight must be allowed their part in literature—even a moment of blindness—but, if the offence is too great, then Bentley's emendation *exeatque* is available (he objected positively to *manet* with *spiritus*, but, as often in Horace, the verb coheres more closely with the nearer subject and the two verbs produced by Bentley sound awkwardly precise, even fussy) or *aestuetque* (based on Cunningham's *aestuatque*—he demanded the indicative).

A point often made against the stanza is that the verbs should not be subjunctive, but indicative since the poet could have had no doubt about the nature of Cerberus. Could he not? The subjunctives should, in fact, be regarded as making a strong claim for Horace's authorship, the ironical doubt of the poet as he reports the usual story about Cerberus is very characteristic of Horace who avoids committing himself factually to the truth of such myths,[1] and this deft touch here serves to inject a faint irony into the whole passage.

But the most generally made objection to the stanza is that *ianitor aulae* is a periphrastic allusion to Cerberus which is spoiled by the pedantic spelling out of the proper name and the long description. This amounts almost to asserting that the poem can do without the stanza. But much poetry could be dispensed with on such a criterion. It is more relevant to notice that if there is a strong stop after *aulae*, then it sounds as if *immanis* goes with *ianitor*: yet *aulae* needs the adjective. But if the sense runs on to *Cerberus*, then a variation on the common order *a b a' b'*[2] is easier to discern.

---

[1] See p. 44 above.

[2] This pattern for arranging two nouns and two adjectives, whether both pairs are interdependent or not, is common in Horace as in all Roman poetry: e.g. ode 4. 17 *tuto ab atris corpore viperis*; 11. 26–7 *inane lymphae dolium . . . pereuntis*, 41–2 *velut nactae vitulos leaenae singulos*; 12. 11–12 *arto latitantem fruticeto . . . aprum*; 16. 35–6 *pinguia Gallicis . . . vellera pascuis*, 39–40 *contracto . . . parva cupidine vectigalia*; 18. 5 *tener pleno . . .*

A stronger argument for the authenticity of the stanza is that the use of a periphrastic phrase followed by the proper name in apposition is a favourite method of introducing epic heroes, and so highly appropriate for this mock-heroic description of Cerberus. Many examples could be quoted from the *Aeneid*, e.g. vii. 678–81:

> nec Praenestinae fundator defuit urbis,
> Volcano genitum pecora inter agrestia regem
> inventumque focis omnis quem credidit aetas,
> Caeculus.

or vii. 761–2:

> Ibat et Hippolyti proles pulcherrima bello
> Virbius, insignem quem mater Aricia misit . . .

The pattern is easily found in *Odes* iii; for instance 4. 60–4 (*Apollo*), or 7. 1–5 (*Gygen*). The effect of such a pattern should be interpreted in literary terms and not as if the author's intention were to convey facts; it is a subtle and potent form of poetic ornament.

Finally, it is worth noticing that, if the doubts about authenticity can be dropped, then the poem conforms to a favourite pattern with Horace in which two major blocks of sense are linked by a centrally placed transitional stanza[1] (of course, the transitional stanza need not be central—see ode 16—and so this cannot be used as an argument for authenticity). Here 1–24 is connected by 25–9 to 30–52. In the course of the transitional stanza the poet's tone alters so that he passes from prayer in 1–24 to narrative in 30–52.

12

Miserarum est neque amori dare ludum neque dulci
mala vino lavere, aut exanimari metuentis
　　patruae verbera linguae.

tibi qualum Cythereae puer ales, tibi telas
operosaeque Minervae studium aufert, Neobule,　　5
　　Liparaei nitor Hebri

haedus anno, 6–7 larga . . . Veneris sodali vina craterae (here the pattern makes it most implausible that *craterae* is genitive and that *veneris sodali* refers to Faunus).
　[1] On this structural pattern, see *Style* F ii.

simul unctos Tiberinis umeros lavit in undis,
eques ipso melior Bellerophonte, neque pugno
    neque segni pede victus;

catus idem per apertum fugientis agitato   10
grege cervos iaculari et celer arto latitantem
    fruticeto excipere aprum.

'It is for lovesick girls neither to give play to love nor to wash
away their miseries with wine—or else faint with terror fearing the
lashes of an uncle's tongue. From you the winged son of Cytherea
steals your basket; from you the beauty of Hebrus from Lipara steals
your loom and your interest in the crafts of Minerva, Neobule, (6)
as soon as he has washed his oiled shoulders in the waters of Tiber,
a horseman better than Bellerophon himself, never beaten through
slowness of fist or foot; (9) he is skilled to spear stags racing over the
open plain when the herd has been frightened, and swift to receive
(the attack of) the boar that tries to hide in the tangled brushwood.'

The unique metre and the perfectly suited subject-matter together carry
this ode along at speed. It commences with a generalization designed to
cover all young women in love (*miser* is almost technical language for the
condition), and then the specific case of Neobule is subsumed under it, by
implication rather than explicitly. Is the poet speaking to Neobule, as
Porphyrio, the best of the ancient commentators on Horace, asserted? If
so, the enthusiastic exposition of the charm and beauty of Hebrus is sur-
prising, which would be more natural in the mouth of Neobule herself.
That she speaks to herself is confirmed by a fragment of a poem in the same
metre by Alcaeus, which Horace must have had in mind.[1] It is clear from the
gender of the person in that poem that the girl speaks—though it is quite
unclear whether she spoke to herself in the second person or whether that
is Horace's invention.

The uncle whose tongue is to be feared if a girl either indulges her love
or drowns her sorrows in drink was proverbial for stern moral censorship.
This opening generalization, followed by *tibi* (4), implies that Neobule
finds herself in a situation where she is only restrained from one or other of
the first two courses by her fear of the third. But she does not need to say
so. Instead, she says (like Landor's young girl) that she cannot mind her

---

[1] See Appendix, no. 1.

wheel, but the sentence is nicely organized so that it moves from general to particular, ending on a long drawn-out testimonial to Hebrus. Her basket (to hold her wool) was taken by Cupid, her loom and her interest in weaving (this element of the sentence—her occupation—moves in the opposite direction from particular to general) by the beauty of Hebrus from Lipara, who excels in swimming, riding, boxing, running, and hunting. The poem ends with her brooding on Hebrus which has taken half of it and so enacts her state of mind.

The girl's name is Greek, but her activity is good Roman practice (Augustus tried to inculcate the virtues of wool-making in the women of his household).[1] The young man's name is Greek, he comes from an island off Sicily: yet his sports are exactly those in which Augustus wished young men of good family to excel,[2] and his swimming is done in the Tiber. Here, as often in Horace, the two cultures meet in an imaginary world as the poet explores, with wit and verve, a common human situation.

13

O fons Bandusiae splendidior vitro
dulci digne mero non sine floribus,
   cras donaberis haedo,
      cui frons turgida cornibus

primis et venerem et proelia destinat—   5
frustra: nam gelidos inficiet tibi
   rubro sanguine rivos
      lascivi suboles gregis.

te flagrantis atrox hora Caniculae
nescit tangere, tu frigus amabile   10
   fessis vomere tauris
      praebes et pecori vago.

[1] Suetonius, *Aug.* 64. 2. Praise of a wife's devotion to wool-making is a frequent theme in Roman literature and on epitaphs (for details, see *Journal of Roman Studies*, 48 [1958], 21, n. 20). For this reason, Horace advises the wife of Ibycus to devote herself to the virtuous pursuit (ode 15 and p. 97 below).

[2] See p. 35 above, n. 2.

fies nobilium tu quoque fontium,
me dicente cavis impositam ilicem
saxis, unde loquaces   15
lymphae desiliunt tuae.

'O spring of Bandusia, more shining than glass, deserving of sweet
wine and flowers, tomorrow you will be presented with a kid whose
forehead, swelling with the tips of horns, gives promise of both love
and battles (5); in vain: for he, the offspring of a playful flock, shall
stain for you your chill waters with his red blood (8).

'The black hour of the flaring Dog-Star knows no means to
touch you: you provide pleasing coolness for tired oxen and the
straggling herd (12).

'You also shall become one of the famous fountains, since I
describe the oak-tree planted over your hollowed rocks from which
your chattering waters jump down.'

The first word indicates the tone of the poem, for *o* in Latin is not, as in
Greek, a mere sign of the vocative case, but signifies an address of emotional
intensity: it is normal in hymnic addresses to gods. The description of the
spring's appearance takes the place of the normal honorific phrases which
are attached to the address in prayers. Here what catches the poet's eye is
not the translucency of the water, but the brightness of the light which it
reflects—as glass reflects light obliquely.[1] There follows (2) a further honorific
phrase which also has the function of setting the poem; for on 13 October
each year Romans celebrated the festival of Fontinalia, throwing flowers
into springs and putting garlands round wells (Varro, *de lingua Latina* vi. 22),
and also—the invariable concomitant of celebration—pouring libations of
wine. The poet declares this humble spring, outside his farmhouse, worthy
of these celebrations, and the next word (*cras*) shows that the poem is being
written on 12 October. But now comes a surprise. The spring will be
honoured with a blood-sacrifice, and the poet's thoughts turn to picture
the tiny animal with its whole life before it—a promise cut short by the
one word *frustra*.[2] Instead he now pictures its red blood staining the spring's
chill waters, a detail which has offended many commentators. The final

---

[1] Callimachus makes the same observation when he describes the sky as 'more
brilliant than glass' (ὑάλοιο φαάντερος οὐρανός) in *Hecale* frag. 238. 16 Pfeiffer. Horace
refers to the more obvious concept of translucency when he describes Fides as *per-
lucidior vitro* (*Odes* i. 18. 16).

[2] On the tonal effect of *frustra*, see *Style* C iii.

two stanzas complete the hymnic form with a series of clauses praising the powers of the spring as if it were a god; the clauses are, as often in prayers, linked by anaphora—*te* ... *tu* ... *tu quoque* ... First, it cannot be harmed by the heat that comes with the Dog Star at the end of July; secondly, it provides refreshment for working oxen and for the thirsty herds. But the third virtue will come to the spring by the poet's grace: since it is his source of inspiration and is described in this poem, it will rank with famous poetic fountains like Castalia, or Hippocrene, or Peirene, celebrated by Greek poets. The poem ends with a perfect evocation of the sound made by the water tumbling down the rocks to form a pool, and they are personified (for they 'chatter' and 'leap'), which is a very suitable idea for a spring that is addressed as if it were a deity, with a life and personality of its own. This final descriptive touch also brings the poem round in full circle to link with the descriptive detail in line 1.[1]

The motif of blood-sacrifice is most surprising in the gentle context of the Fontinalia and needs further consideration. It is quite different when Ovid says (*Fasti* iii. 300) that king Numa, trying to capture Faunus and Picus, sacrificed a sheep and placed wine by a fountain at which they used to drink. In an otherwise comparable Greek epigram by Leonidas of Tarentum (*Palatine Anthology* ix. 326),[2] a wayfarer dedicates a cup to a spring at which he has drunk. There is indeed a whole series of Greek epigrams in which animals are dedicated to deities, but these are wild animals and their hunters make the dedications. This fact distinguishes them from Horace's goat, and also the fact that their death has none of the pathos which Horace arouses. There are two types of poetry where this pathetic sentiment is found: one is a long series of epitaphs, Greek and Roman, on pet animals which purport to be written by their owners or an interested observer; these again are clearly different from this ode. The other is Virgil's *Georgics* where the poet achieves pathos and humour by treating the animals in human terms. Where Horace differs is in arousing pathos for an animal which, by his own free decision, he destines to death. This cannot avoid being somewhat macabre, especially when the poet goes on to evoke the visual effect of the red blood seeping into the chill water. But the use of the motif will be misjudged unless the detached, slightly callous irony of the pathos is appreciated: the mock-heroic combination of *et venerem et proelia* and the deliberately dropped *frustra* create a tone that is alien to the sympathetic Virgil.

The use of this motif needs to be considered in relation to the ode's structure. If Greek analogies are sought, they will be found in epigrams

---

[1] On the structure of 'ring-composition', see *Style* F 1.   [2] See Appendix, no. 9.

written to make dedications. These are short and simple, but this ode is surprisingly complex. First, its very setting is complex and the reader is left to work out the clues in line 2 for himself. Secondly, the thematic material is complex. For instance, the last stanza can be viewed as an assertion by Horace of the worth of his poetry. But that is only one aspect of it. It is formally accommodated to the hymnic treatment of a deity's virtues; and it is also related to the first stanza not only by the fact that the description of the spring's water looks back to line 1, but also because the first stanza promises the spring a sacrifice of a material sort, while the poem which is the subject of the last stanza is really a further act of homage to the spring. The virtue of the sacrifice-motif is that it not only adds another considerable element to the complexity, but it also introduces an emotional pathos that goes out beyond the main movement of the poem and adds a new dimension to it. In this deft handling of a complex of themes Horace creates a new and major poetic form out of Greek epigram.[1]

14

Herculis ritu modo dictus, o plebs,
morte venalem petiisse laurum
Caesar Hispana repetit penatis
    victor ab ora.

unico gaudens mulier marito   5
prodeat iustis operata divis,
et soror clari ducis et decorae
    supplice vitta

virginum matres iuvenumque nuper
sospitum. vos, o pueri et puellae   10
iam virum expertae, male ominatis[2]
    parcite verbis.

hic dies vere mihi festus atras
eximet curas: ego nec tumultum
nec mori per vim metuam tenente   15
    Caesare terras.

[1] On this feature, see *Style* F III.   [2] On this reading, see pp. 94–6 below.

i pete unguentum, puer, et coronas
et cadum Marsi memorem duelli,
Spartacum si qua potuit vagantem
    fallere testa.   20

dic et argutae properet Neaerae
murreum nodo cohibere crinem;
si per invisum mora ianitorem
    fiet, abito.

lenit albescens animos capillus   25
litium et rixae cupidos protervae:
non ego hoc ferrem calidus iuventa
    consule Planco.

'Lately reported, o people of the city, to have sought, after the manner of Hercules, the laurel that is bought with death, Caesar is making for his home, a victor from the coast of Spain (4). Let his wife, rejoicing in her one and only husband, process after sacrificing to the just gods, and the sister of our famous leader and, adorned with suppliant garland, mothers of virgins and of young men who were lately saved. You, o boys and you, girls (10) that have experienced a husband, refrain from ill-omened words.

'This day, truly festal for me, shall take my dark worries away: I shall fear neither revolution nor death by violence so long as Caesar controls the world (16).

'Go, find ointment, slave, and garlands of flowers and a cask of wine that remembers the Marsian war—if any bottle was able to escape the notice of the ravaging Spartacus (20). And bid sweet-voiced Neaera hurry to put up her light-brown hair in a knot; if interference shall be made by the hateful janitor, come away. Greying hair soothes a spirit once eager for disputes and heated quarrelling (26): I would not have put up with this, hot with youth when Plancus was consul.'

In the first part of the ode (1–12), the poet adopts a formal pose which was often used by Hellenistic Greek poets: it is that of a herald or public announcer describing or prescribing a complex ceremony. Here the poet speaks to the people of Rome and gives directions for celebrating the return of Augustus from Spain in 24 B.C., where, for nearly three years, he had been directing operations against the Cantabri, ancient enemies of Rome;[1] in fact, the war was not completed till 19 B.C., but the poet treats the return of Augustus as indicative of victory. The form of address *o plebs* (where *o* indicates emotional excitement)[2] is unparalleled, and the poet has ventured it to suggest that the whole populace is gathered to hear the announcement: these are the common people of Rome who will only be spectators of the ceremony. Horace never treats Augustus as a god; instead he associates him with gods and heroes.[3] Here the choice of Hercules is relevant in two respects: Hercules was reckoned one of the great benefactors of mankind for ridding the earth of dangerous monsters, and one of these was Geryon in Spain—after which Hercules returned through Italy, past the future site of Rome (see the story of his fight with Cacus in *Aeneid* viii. 185–275). Augustus has risked his life to achieve victory and now returns home (symbolized by the household gods, the Penates): this completes the announcement to the populace and the poet now prescribes the details of the reception (5–12).

First, Augustus' wife, Livia, is to come forth, after sacrifice to gods[4] who are just because they have returned her husband safe and victorious. She is given an honorific description (5) which is a circumlocution for *univira*; this was a term applied to women who married once and once only (i.e. they did not remarry after divorce or widowhood), and such women were given certain privileges. The concept was revived by Augustus' efforts for moral reform and legislation,[5] but in Livia's case it was purely honorific since she had been married to Ti. Claudius Nero whom she divorced to marry Octavian in 38 B.C. (as he divorced Scribonia). But it was a compliment (as when in 9 B.C. the Senate voted her the *ius trium liberorum*

---

[1] Carthaginian influence in Spain had drawn the Romans in during the latter part of the third century B.C. Organized resistance against Rome seemed to be ended by the capture of Numantia in 133 B.C., but over a century of sporadic war followed. The Augustan settlement was decisive and Spain became one of the most deeply Romanized parts of the empire, making a distinct contribution to Roman culture.

[2] See p. 88 above, on ode 13. 1.

[3] See p. 42 above, n. 1.

[4] Half of the manuscripts give *sacris*, but if this is accepted then *iustis* means 'correct' and the poet is prescribing how Livia is to perform her sacrifice ('with correct rites'). Thereby, however, far too much emphasis is laid on the poet's pose as a master of ceremonies and far too little on the fact that this is a poetic pose which enables him too to celebrate the return of Augustus. If *divis* is read, with the other half of the manuscripts and Porphyrio, then the poet himself gives thanks in the word *iustis* under the guise of ordering Livia to do so; this has real point, unlike *sacris*.

[5] See p. 5 above and commentary, especially on odes 6 and 24.

in spite of her having only two children, neither by Augustus), as pleasing to Augustus as to her. Secondly, Augustus' sister, Octavia, is to come forth; and thirdly married women, the mothers of soldiers who have returned with Augustus and also of young girls. Here the poet deftly suggests all those who will be most pleased by the return: the mothers, their soldier sons, and the young girls for whom the return will mean marriage. He has omitted two categories, however, and he now picks them up in his next words (10–12) which are ostensibly a request for the avoidance of ill-omened words:[1] he addresses the request to young boys (i.e. brothers of the soldiers) and young married girls[2] (i.e. wives of the soldiers), so that *virgines* contrast with *puellae iam virum expertae* much as *pueri* with *iuvenes nuper sospites* and the two pairs are chiastically arranged. In this way a vast crowd of people, all with different reasons for rejoicing, is brought to life by the poet's pretence to be giving instructions, and their noisy, excited chattering is suggested.

The second half of the ode (17–28) represents the poet in another pose—that of ordering preparations for a private party—but, as often in odes which consist of an uneven number of stanzas, a central stanza makes the transition from one to the other.[3] Here (13–16), after completing his instructions for public celebration, the poet expresses his own feelings: the day will be a day of celebration for him too since it has removed his worries that Augustus, the one guarantee against a recurrence of civil war (suggested by *tumultus* and *mori per vim*), might be killed in Spain.

The orders for the poet's private party are given to his slave (*puer*) and they are for scented balsam (for putting on the hair), flowers (to make garlands), wine and a girl (to provide songs—*argutae*—and make love). But the poet lingers over the wine with curious insistence: he specifies the year—approximately 90 B.C. when all Italy was convulsed in the Social War—but doubts if any bottle escaped the ravages of Spartacus during the terrible Slave War of 73 B.C. He gives a pretty picture of Neaera coiling her light brown hair on top of her head, but he is not too anxious for her presence—if the porter at her house, bribed by some other lover to bar access to her, is troublesome, the slave is not to bother. And the poet's thoughts turn to a time, nearly twenty years earlier, when he was young and hot-tempered—he would not have taken 'No' for an answer then. He marks that year precisely with the date *consule Planco*: it was the year 42 B.C. when Horace, inflamed by Brutus with talk of liberty, had fought on his side at Philippi

---

[1] See ode 1. 1–4 and commentary.
[2] Horace uses *puellae* in this sense in ode 22. 2.
[3] On this structure, see *Style* F 11.

and lost a battle in which the nobility of Rome was virtually wiped out by Antony and Octavian. So, although the poet is ostensibly ordering preparations for a private drinking-party of his own to celebrate Augustus' return, his thoughts cannot stop harping on the most terrible years that Rome has known in recent history and on troubles from which only the dominance of Augustus has been able to save the people. So the party— no less than the public celebration which the poet purported to be prescribing—is a formal invention: it gives Horace the opportunity for reflecting on the political situation which affects the lives of the community as a whole no less than the private life of the poet, less easily moved to anger—or love—now, but happier than in those far-off, dangerous days. The poem closes with a purely reflective stanza which carries the poet away from present celebrations into ambiguous thoughts that combine regret for lost youth with relief at dangers past.

The problem of (11) male ominatis

As printed above, line 11 contains a hiatus ((*iām vĭr(um) ēxpērtāe mălĕ | ōmĭnātīs*). Attempts have been made to emend the first three words to eliminate the hiatus; these can be dismissed because they involve altering the meaning (on which see the commentary). Two other solutions need consideration.

(i) *male nominatis*: this is what all except two manuscripts read, together with the lemma of Porphyrio (though his comment indicates that he had *male ominatis* in his text of Horace). Many modern texts print it, but it is hard to think it Latin—let alone the writing of an elegant and subtle poet. It is sometimes defended as the Latin for Greek δυσώνυμα—a hopeless defence, for no Greek would say δυσώνυμα ἔπη (as Horace is required to say *male nominatis . . . verbis*). The phrase could mean 'incorrectly parsed words' (i.e. wrongly called e.g. 'verb, adjective, noun, etc.'), but that does not suit. It cannot mean 'ill-mentioned words' in the sense of 'words which, if mentioned, would be ill mentioned', for *nominare* does not mean simply 'mention'. When Cato addresses the senate in reply to Caesar and says (Sallust, *Catiline* 52. 11) *hic mihi quisquam mansuetudinem et misericordiam nominat?* he means 'Does someone use the words "clemency" and "pity" to me (of the course which Caesar advises)?' For he goes on: *iampridem equidem nos vera vocabula rerum amisimus*: 'we have long since lost the true names for things'.

(ii) *male inominatis*: this was Bentley's emendation. The word *inominatus* occurs once elsewhere in Latin: Horace, *Epodes* 16. 38 *inominata perpremat cubilia*. But this emendation will not do. (*a*) The meaning of *inominatus* is not 'ill-omened' but 'un-omened' (like *inauspicatus* at ode 6. 10); at *Epodes* 16. 38 the beds would be 'un-omened', i.e. it would not be a state of honourable matrimony (for which omens were needed: Virgil, *Aeneid* i. 346, Prop. iii. 20. 24). (*b*) The intensive *male* (it negatives adjectives of approval, intensifies those of disapproval) is quite inappropriate here, for it is naturally not used with negative adjectives (the two instances of Catullus 10. 33 *insulsa male* and Sulpicia ap. Tibullum iv. 10. 2 *male inepta* prove this rule, since they are not mere negative adjectives from *salsus* and *aptus* but have positive meanings in their own right) and its tone would be colloquially emotional.[1] In any case, it is most unlikely that Horace would have thought of saying 'avoid *very* ill-omened words'; this would be weak and silly— *male* ought to have its full technical sense here.

(iii) There seems a strong probability that Horace did actually write *male ominatis*. There is one other hiatus in the *Odes* at i. 28. 24 *ossibus et capiti | inhumato*. There are similarly isolated examples of hiatus like *male ominatis* in other poets. Catullus seems to have written at 114. 6 *saltum laudemus, dummodo | ipse egeat*. At *Eclogues* 2. 53 Virgil wrote *addam cerea pruna |—honos erit huic quoque pomo* and at *Aeneid* i. 405 *et vera incessu patuit dea. | ille ubi matrem* (at xii. 648 he may have written, as the manuscripts suggest, *sancta ad vos anima | atque istius inscia culpae*). Those in Virgil are alleviated by pauses in sense. But the fact is that these poets just very occasionally allowed a surprising hiatus in their writing. It is useless to speculate on the poet's state of mind when he did it (e.g. was it inadvertence?). What seems likely is that times must come to the best poets when the essential rightness of the words that have come to them outweighs their prejudice against hiatus.[2] When that happened they will have been glad to find similar occasions in admired earlier writers—and analogies to those in Virgil can be found in Homer; Greek metrical practice also provides analogies to *Odes* i. 28. 24—so much so that it is often called a 'Greek' hiatus (as if that explained it). There are also analogies to the hiatus between a short vowel and a long vowel as in *male ominatis*. For instance, Callimachus writes frag. 59. 20 πέμψε δέ οἱ τὸν ὀρῆα, τίεν δέ ἑ ὡς ἕνα πηῶν. Quintilian, who minimizes the offence of hiatus, seems to say (*Inst. Orat.* ix. 4. 34) that hiatus caused by a short preceding a long vowel is not serious, but his precise meaning is very unclear. At any rate Horace did permit some surprising hiatus in his other works: for instance, *Satires* i. 9. 17 *cĭrcŭmăgī*,

[1] If *male insani* (and not *male sani*) is the correct reading at Seneca, *controv.* 2. 1. 8, it is to be taken as underlining the extravagance of the emotional rhetorical question.
[2] Poets do write isolated oddities (and Homer nods): see, for instance, the evidence on *eius*, p. 84 above, or—another unique oddity—*cumque* in *Odes* i. 32. 15.

where the coherence of *circum* and *agi* is as close as that of *male ominatis* and where the only apparent excuse is that the metre requires the word to be pronounced with a hiatus.

15

Uxor pauperis Ibyci,
tandem nequitiae fige modum tuae
   famosisque laboribus:
maturo propior desine funeri

   inter ludere virgines   5
et stellis nebulam spargere candidis.
   non, si quid Pholoen satis,
et te, Chlori, decet: filia rectius

   expugnat iuvenum domos,
pulso Thyias uti concita tympano.   10
   illam cogit amor Nothi
lascivae similem ludere capreae:

   te lanae prope nobilem
tonsae Luceriam, non citharae decent
   nec flos purpureus rosae   15
nec poti vetulam faece tenus cadi.

'Wife of hard-working Ibycus, do at last set a limit to your flightiness and your scandalous efforts: nearer to a death at the normal age, cease to play among unmarried girls (5) and cast a cloud over such bright stars. Just because something is right for Pholoe, it is not also right for you, Chloris: your daughter, with more propriety, tries to take young men's homes by storm, like a Bacchante intoxicated by the beating of the tambourine (10). Love for Nothus compels her to play like a frisky doe: for you wool shorn near famous Luceria is suitable, not lyres nor the crimson flower of the rose (15) nor wine-casks drunk right down to the dregs—you old woman.'

The poet addresses a married woman, using the name of her husband and reserving her own name for a dramatic moment. She must cease her misconduct (2–3) and her play among young girls (which only casts a cloud over their brightness) since she is closer to a death that could not be designated premature (than to them). Now comes the woman's name: because her daughter can do something with propriety, it does not mean that Chloris can (7–8). Pholoe assaults the doors of young men like a frenzied Bacchante —well, she has more justification (10–12). The poet does not convey approval of Pholoe, but understanding; for Chloris, if she does the same, utter condemnation. Pholoe is in love with Nothus, so she behaves like a playful kid (11–12). For Chloris it should be wool-making (and the poet names one of the great wool-producing areas of Italy, Luceria)[1] and not (as for Pholoe) music and roses and deep drinking.

The names are all Greek: Ibycus was the name of a sixth-century Greek lyric poet, famous for his libidinous life and verse, while Nothus was the Greek for 'Bastard' (especially the son of a free man and a slave woman). Both names are no doubt chosen with deliberate humour, and the situation seems to be one of Greek fantasy. But the sudden appearance of Luceria is surprising and strikes a note of Roman reality which the reader now recognizes was really inherent in the first word of the ode—*uxor*, and the moral tone implicit in *pauperis* (1)[2] is the same as that in the recommendation to wool-making. The value of the poem lies in this humorous interaction of the two cultures, Greek and Roman, of the two age-groups in women— young and middle-aged, of the husband's poverty (and his name) and the behaviour of the females of the family, and in the poet's lingering pleasure over the delights which he condemns for Chloris—for it is no accident that the last three lines of the poem linger over the details of a luxurious drinking-party. Such activities are naturally appropriate for the poet.

16

Inclusam Danaen turris aenea
robustaeque fores et vigilum canum
tristes excubiae munierant satis
nocturnis ab adulteris,

---

[1] See p. 87 above, n. 1.
[2] See p. 34 above, n. 1.

H

si non Acrisium virginis abditae   5
custodem pavidum Iuppiter et Venus
risissent: fore enim tutum iter et patens
    converso in pretium deo.

aurum per medios ire satellites
et perrumpere amat saxa potentius   10
ictu fulmineo: concidit auguris
    Argivi domus ob lucrum

demersa exitio; diffidit urbium
portas vir Macedo et subruit aemulos
reges muneribus; munera navium   15
    saevos illaqueant duces.

crescentem sequitur cura pecuniam
maiorumque fames: iure perhorrui
late conspicuum tollere verticem,
    Maecenas, equitum decus.   20

quanto quisque sibi plura negaverit,
ab dis plura feret: nil cupientium
nudus castra peto et transfuga divitum
    partis linquere gestio,

contemptae dominus splendidior rei   25
quam si quidquid arat impiger Apulus
occultare meis dicerer horreis,
    magnas inter opes inops;

purae rivus aquae silvaque iugerum
paucorum et segetis certa fides meae   30
fulgentem imperio fertilis Africae
    fallit sorte beatior.

quamquam nec Calabrae mella ferunt apes
nec Laestrygonia Bacchus in amphora
languescit mihi nec pinguia Gallicis   35
    crescunt vellera pascuis,

importuna tamen pauperies abest
nec, si plura velim, tu dare deneges.
contracto melius parva cupidine
    vectigalia porrigam,   40

quam si Mygdoniis regnum Alyattei
campis continuem; multa petentibus
desunt multa: bene est, cui deus obtulit
    parca quod satis est manu.

'A tower of brass and oaken doors and the grim watchfulness of
unsleeping guard-dogs had kept the imprisoned Danaë safe from
adulterers by night (4), if only Juppiter and Venus had not laughed
at Acrisius, the frightened keeper of the hidden girl: for a way, a
safe and open way, would be found for the god turned into a bribe.
Gold is wont to make its way right through the midst of body-
guards and to burst asunder stone walls more powerfully (10) than a
flash of lightning: the house of the Argive augur fell, sunk in destruc-
tion, for gain; the man of Macedon split the gates of cities and sub-
verted rival kings with bribes; bribes ensnare the savage captains
of ships (16).

'Worry and hunger for more keep pace with increasing wealth:
justifiably I have shrunk from raising my head in conspicuous pride,
Maecenas, glory of the knights (20).

'The more each man denies himself, the more he will get from the
gods: stripped of possessions, I seek the camp of those who desire
nothing and I am eager to be a deserter from the lines of the wealthy,
more splendid as the owner of a despised estate (25) than if I were
reputed to hide away in my barns the produce of all that the hard-
working Apulian ploughs, needy amidst great riches; a river of
pure water and a wood of a few acres and the sure reliability of
my cornfield (30) make me happier than a famous governor of fertile
Africa—though he does not realize it. Although no Calabrian bees
bring honey, nor does Bacchus grow mellow in a Laestrygonian

cask,[1] nor do fleeces grow rich for me in Gallic pastures (36), yet pinching poverty is absent and, if I were to wish more, you would not refuse it to me. I shall do better to stretch my income by contracting my wants (40) than if I were to combine the kingdom of Alyattes with the Mygdonian plains; to those who want much, much is lacking: it is well with him to whom god has given, with thrifty hand, what is enough.'

The poem opens with a striking picture of Danaë locked in a tower of brass, with oak doors and savage guard-dogs all round; then the frightened Acrisius (her father and king of Argos) appears (terrified by the oracle which foretold that his daughter's son would kill him), followed instantly by the mocking gods. Here, in *risissent*, Acrisius' plans crash. If the poet had written *munivissent* this would have happened already in line 3, but there he maintains the deception (which also caught Acrisius) by using the pluperfect indicative which leaves open the possibility that the plan succeeded until the door is finally closed by the pluperfect subjunctive *risissent*.[1] This is a literary effect which is independent of the fact that the reader naturally knows the outcome of so famous a story. The reason for the gods' laughter is expressed in the accusative and infinitive (7-8), which represents it as what they said to one another. Here a chill tone of moralizing enters the poem for it now becomes clear that the poet has only used the romantic story of Danaë to illustrate the power of money and that he relies on a rationalizing interpretation of the legend which explained the shower of gold as bribery of Danaë's guards. Greek Stoic philosophers were prone to this type of heavy-handed interpretation, but it should be noticed that the poet has still left an element of mystery in the story: 'the god turned into a bribe' is an imaginative idea, because it leaves the important activity of the god still obscure and he is still a god. Horace stops well short of debunking the myth. The idea of *pretium* (8) is now taken up in a slightly different form, *aurum* (9), and a generalization depicts gold finding a way through a tyrant's bodyguard to kill him and breaking open stone walls of prisons, like lightning: here the ideas move out to take in the strange political system of tyranny such as Greece and the Near East knew. There follow three examples: the whole house of Amphiaraus was destroyed by Eriphyle's acceptance of a necklace to persuade her husband to go on the expedition of the Seven against Thebes (for he, prophet that he was, knew that he would die)—her son slew her and was himself exiled. This complex legend is recalled in a few telling words (11-13). Next comes the example of Philip

---

[1] i.e. from Formiae (see p. 105).   [2] On this, see *Style* B 1.

of Macedon who boasted that he could capture any city up to which he could drive a mule loaded with gold (Cicero, *ad Att.* i. 16. 12). This brief account (13-15) of a master of the technique of bribery for military and political ends is completed with the word *muneribus* (15), which is instantly repeated in a different case—*munera* (15)—to make a link with the next picture of pirates falling victims to bribery. There may here be a reference to the case of Menas, admiral of Sextus Pompeius, who was twice enticed to the side of Octavian with bribes:[1] but, if so, Horace has deliberately generalized it (in contrast to the two previous examples) to constitute a universal rule. In this form it makes an excellent and allusive conclusion to the first section of the poem.

This ode is contructed on a slight variant of the system whereby two equal blocks of sense are connected by a transitional stanza.[2] The difference here is that the blocks are unequal (1-16, 21-44), and also that the gap between is particularly wide. The first block (1-16) expresses the power of wealth, and the second (21-44) the idea that the best wealth is inner content; also the first block is expressed impersonally and objectively, but the second in terms of the poet's own life and experience. The transition is made first by a generalization (17-18): wealth creates desire for more wealth—and so anxiety (the relevance of the generalization is that from 1-16 the conclusion might be drawn that the more wealth the more power, but wealth has, in fact, a built-in disadvantage . . .). Now it would be ridiculous and immodest if the poet simply introduced himself into this contrast, for it would imply that the capacity existed in him to achieve vast wealth. So he says that he has been right to recoil from trying to cut a figure in the world, and he addresses these words to Maecenas whom he calls 'glory of the knights'—alluding to the well-known fact that Maecenas kept refusing a more eminent situation. By this means, the poet shifts the emphasis from any suggestion that he himself could become famous and wealthy to the actual fact that Maecenas refused any such distinctions. Yet the effect of the stanza has been to introduce the poet's own life, and this can now come to the forefront in the second block (21-44).

The poet starts again, as it were, with a new generalization (21-2): the more a man denies himself, the more the gods will give him. This is a more modest rubric for the poet to appear beneath, and so he represents himself as a deserter from the army of the wealthy to that of men who desire nothing. He does not mean that he had once been wealthy, but that any man can choose a side for himself, and in doing that he rejects the other

---

[1] For the story of this freedman, see *Cambridge Ancient History*, x. 56-60.
[2] For this structure, see *Style* F II.

side, and, furthermore, that most men (like Horace) find that they have both desires and possessions so that they start by being naturally on the side of the wealthy. The poet now finds two paradoxical ways of expressing his happiness in modest living. The first is negative, or, rather, it forestalls a critic's point of view (25-8): he feels more distinguished as the owner of an estate that others despise than if men were to say of him (27 *dicerer*) that he stored in his barns all the corn produced by hard-working Apulian farmers (chosen not because Apulia was famous for corn but because it was the poet's own homeland and its inhabitants were proverbial as hard workers), for then he would have great wealth but would really be poor. Then he puts this viewpoint positively by describing his satisfaction in his property (29-30): the man who owns so much of proverbially rich Africa that he thinks himself a king, or who is proconsul of that province, does not realize the greater happiness of Horace's lot. This latter comparison (31-2) is expressed with a brevity that is obscure but impressive: it is the poet's property—not himself—that is said to be happier in its lot and it 'escapes the notice' (*fallit* is used as Greek λανθάνειν) of the man who 'shines' (both in his own estimation and others') 'with the command of fertile Africa'.[1] Now the poet approaches the same idea from a different point of view and with a new emphasis: though he has not famous possessions (33-6), yet serious poverty does not afflict him (37)—and, in any case, Maecenas would always be ready to help (38). The poet will do better, however, to increase his income (40) by reducing his need for expenditure (39) than if he were to add the kingdom of Lydia (of which Croesus, son of Alyattes, was king) to the plains of Phrygia (of which proverbially gold-bearing lands Mygdon was king). Now the poet has reached a point where he can sum up his view in two more contrasted generalizations: (i) if men search for much, they lack much (i.e. they feel the lack of much); and, conversely (ii) it is well for the man to whom god has given sparingly what is enough (i.e. what he feels to be enough for him).

This is a conclusion which is surprisingly remote from the opening of the poem. There the leading idea was the inordinate power of money: yet the

[1] Africa was a very rich Roman province, developed and exploited by Roman capital. It was under the command of a proconsul. Horace's language moves in the direction of referring to this official in the words *imperio* and *sorte*. But the proconsul, of course, in no sense owned Africa, so either the poet has chosen the proconsul as a man who has achieved the height of political ambition (both in the office he has attained and in the very important province which he now governs) in Roman eyes, or he is using the Roman political terms to express the sense of importance of a (Roman) man who owns great tracts of rich Africa. The former interpretation has the advantage of doing more precise justice to the technical terms and of making the poet renounce not only great possessions (which he has already done) but also political ambition.

poem ends with the idea that the man who has the least possible money, the minimum needed for his life, is the happiest. This ingenuity and un-expectedness of its structure is the best feature of the poem. The stream of ideas is diverted several times by a surprising and dexterous use of generali-zations. In spite of this the poem scarcely comes alive. The ideal of the quiet life was one of Horace's most moving inspirations, expressed auto-biographically with a depth of poetical conviction. Yet his entrance into this poem fails to set it on fire; it is as if he were using himself—as he uses every other pictorial effect in the poem—to illustrate a generalization. The result is that even his self-portrait rings false: there is a contradiction between (23) *nudus* and the list of possessions in 29 ff., and the sentimental note of (30) *segetis certa fides meae* is false. Worse is the fact that the poet makes his own *pauperies* sound smug and cushioned. This is because he says tha Maecenas will always give him more if he asks. The motives for this as-sertion are twofold: (i) it expresses gratitude to his friend and patron; and (ii) it makes clear that his *pauperies* is purely voluntary—a fact which should impress the reader with its spiritual value. But the motives are mis-calculated and the effect misfires, mainly because the poet's tone is too didactic—it is too close to that of the preacher—and such a tone is ill suited to express an inner conviction. In poems like 1 and 24, where the poet ex-presses a similar point of view, the poet's inner conviction comes through to the reader as a by-product of the poetic vision: he sees his own society, or human life as a whole, in a series of contrasting pictures and the concept which unifies them, the generalization or sermon-text, does not need to be hammered home. In 16, however, the poet starts from the generalization in each case and his poetry degenerates into a means of illustrating it.

17

Aeli vetusto nobilis ab Lamo
(quando et priores hinc Lamias ferunt
    denominatos et nepotum
        per memores genus omne fastus,

auctore ab illo ducis originem,   5
qui Formiarum moenia dicitur
    princeps et innantem Maricae
        litoribus tenuisse Lirim

late tyrannus) cras foliis nemus
multis et alga litus inutili   10
    demissa tempestas ab Euro
        sternet, aquae nisi fallit augur

annosa cornix. dum potes, aridum
compone lignum: cras Genium mero
    curabis et porco bimestri   15
        cum famulis operum solutis.

'Aelius, of noble descent from ancient Lamus (since they allege that
both the earlier Lamiae derived their name from him and then the
whole line of descendants throughout the memorial records, you
derive your origin from that first founder (5) who is said to have been
the first to control the fortifications of Formiae and the river Liris
flooding over the shores of Marica, tyrant of all that region), to-
morrow a storm hurled down by the east wind will strew the grove
with a litter of leaves and the shore with useless seaweed (11), if the
aged crow, the prophet of rain, does not deceive me. While you
can, gather dry firewood: tomorrow, in company with your servants
released from work, you shall refresh your guardian-spirit with wine
and a two-month-old pig.'

The poem opens on an elevated and honorific note, with a touch of mystery
about it for its meaning is not immediately clear (*nobilis* in the late Republic
signified a man whose family had held the consulship, but the word could
also—as here—mean 'famous'). The mysterious opening gives ground for
the long explanatory parenthesis (see *Style* B III) which follows (2–9). The
poet claims that tradition derives the family of Aelii Lamiae from Lamus,
king of the Laestrygonians, the savage tribe with whom Odysseus had the
unpleasant adventure described in *Odyssey* x. 81 ff. (he claims the evi-
dence of the *fasti* which were officially the lists of magistrates at Rome, but
here, informally, mean family records). This information is offered in
solemn antiquarian style, but now (5–9) the poet comes to the real evidence
on which he bases the assertion: the Aelii Lamiae have an estate near
Formiae and this was the region where the legendary Lamus was said to
have been king. The poet creates a perfect word-picture of the marshy
valley by which the Liris enters the sea at Minturnae where the local goddess
Marica had a temple.

The poet now claims (in virtue of his special powers of inspiration and prophecy) to know that a storm will come tomorrow, for he has observed the behaviour of a crow (proverbially both old and an infallible weather-sign). He gives instructions (in virtue of his status as poet) to gather fire-wood, but then moves into the more polite future tense (which can still have a prescriptive force in such contexts) to foretell a holiday pleasantly spent, with the farm-labourers unable to work in the rain. The Genius was a man's inner spirit which was born with him and so was the focus of celebration on a birthday. The language throughout is solemn and elevated (*operum solutis* is an imitation of a Greek construction).

The man addressed was probably L. Aelius Lamia, destined to be consul in A.D. 3. His father was a very wealthy banker, a friend of Cicero and praetor in 43 B.C., and the family was clearly important. Horace seems to have been on close terms with the son: he mentions him in *Odes* i. 26 and 36 and in *Epistles* i. 14. This ode contains two elements: the legendary family descent and the preparations for a celebration. The descent from Lamus may well be an actual invention of the poet or, at least, a joke shared between him and his friend, for it looks as if the poet had to extend the area dominated by Lamus from Formiae (about which there was this legend) to Minturnae, ten miles away; and one may guess that this was necessitated by the family estate's being at Minturnae, not Formiae. At any rate, this descent is a carefully worked-out joke, a parody of a craze which Roman families had for tracing their ancestry back to Trojans (Varro wrote a work called *de familiis Troianis*). The elevated language in which the poet presents this nonsense is a perfect vehicle for his mock-solemn tone—and the whole passage exhibits a close intimacy and friendship with his addressee. The second element is the ostensible occasion for the poem, and it is one which Horace used often in many forms: the prescription of a celebration. Its function is to create the scene and atmosphere of the poem: a landscape of country and sea, and the quiet pleasures of a simple life.

18

Faune, Nympharum fugientum amator,
per meos finis et aprica rura
lenis incedas abeasque parvis
    aequus alumnis,

si tener pleno cadit haedus anno,   5
larga nec desunt Veneris sodali
vina craterae, vetus ara multo
    fumat odore;

ludit herboso pecus omne campo,
cum tibi Nonae redeunt Decembres,   10
festus in pratis vacat otioso
    cum bove pagus,

inter audaces lupus errat agnos,
spargit agrestis tibi silva frondis,
gaudet invisam pepulisse fossor   15
    ter pede terram.

'Faunus, lover of the nymphs who run from you, come gently through my domain and sunny countryside and depart again kindly to my small nurslings, seeing that a kid is slaughtered at the completion of the year (5) and wine in plenty is not lacking to the mixing-bowl, the companion of Venus: the ancient altar is smoking with much incense; the whole herd plays over the grassy plain, as the Nones of December return in your honour (10), the village in festivity takes its ease in the meadows, together with the ox on holiday too, the wolf wanders amongst lambs that are unafraid, the rustic wood throws down its leaves in your honour (14), the ditcher rejoices to pound the hated earth three times with his foot.'

From the outset the poem is in the form of a hymn to Faunus. He was an Italian rural deity, the protector of flocks—especially against wolves. But when the poet adds, as an honorific address, *nympharum fugientum amator*, he both thinks of him in terms of the Greek god Pan[1] and also introduces a tone of joking in the word *fugientum*.[2] It is an ancient formula of prayer when he goes on to prescribe (2–4) how the god shall come and—just as important—go away, because gods could be dangerous to mortals, especially a god whose function as protector against wolves suggested that he had something of the wolf about him. The next stanza functions as that part of the prayer which specified the tribute that the worshipper, for his part,

---

[1] Compare the treatment of Diana in ode 22 (see commentary).
[2] For the sudden flash of humour, compare ode 1. 33–4 and see *Style* C 1.

would contribute, and the *si*-clauses have less the force of a condition to be fulfilled in certain circumstances than of an assurance that they are, of course, being fulfilled: so the meaning of *si* is nearer to 'since'. There will be a sacrifice of a young kid (5) and libations of wine (6–7): the mixing-bowl (*cratera*) from which the wine is taken is called 'the companion of Venus'[1] both because wine and love go proverbially together, and also because the day will be a festive holiday and appropriate for love-making. The final picture (7–8) of the smoking altar is set apart from the other two by asyndeton because it functions not so much as a specific act of honour to the god as a detail which moves on to describe the sacrifice as already under way.[2] So it leads straight into the final two stanzas which go out from the strict prayer-form into a more general description of the festival; but, at the same time, the poet keeps the prayer firmly in mind with repeated *tibi* (10) ... *tibi* (14) ... The stanza (9–12) is a perfect description of a village on holiday, with the nice detail *otioso cum bove* (for in the ancient world, working animals on a farm were oxen, not horses). The poet now seems to move out into a magical world (13–14), but the two ideas are simply means of regarding quite ordinary features of the occasion and expressing them in ways (appropriate to each) which are more honorific to the god: a central intention of the festival was to obtain protection for the new-born lambs[3] from wolves and the poet expresses this optatively by a concrete picture of a wolf prowling among lambs which feel no need to fear him; secondly, it is now late in the year (the Faunalia was held on 5 December— *nonae Decembres*) and the trees have shed their leaves, a fact which the poet professes to regard as a deliberate act of homage to the god. The poem ends with a splendidly calculated detail, straight out of rustic life (as in a painting by Bruegel), of a ploughman dancing the triple-beat rhythm so clumsily that he seems simply to be expressing pent-up hatred for the soil (over which he labours so long) by kicking it.

The poem is an excellent example of the way in which a poetic form can be set to do a specific task that seems at first to be alien to it. Here Horace has used a prayer to accommodate an impressionistic description of a rustic

---

[1] See p. 84 above, n. 2.

[2] On this structure, see *Style* B II.

[3] Pliny, *Natural History* viii. 187, giving advice on sheep-breeding, says that sheep conceive between 13 May and 23 July and that their period of gestation is 150 days (this is accurate). This means that lambs were born from about mid-October to mid-December. So there will have been plenty of new-born lambs by the Faunalia. It is worth adding that Pliny (*N.H.* viii. 200) records she-goats as conceiving in November and the kids as born in March; a kid would therefore be a suitable animal to think of killing and eating in December (5 *tener* . . . *haedus*).

festival, catching the very essence of an occasion that combines worship—
as the ancient world knew it—with simple enjoyment of a holiday by simple
people. It is hard to assess what contribution the form here makes to the
poem as a whole; but the fact that it is a prayer creates an emotional element
which would otherwise be lacking. The sense of a religious occasion, which
is fundamental to the poem, brings with it something of the feeling of a
relationship between man and forces in the world outside him that lie
outside the scope of rational explanation. The poet does not need to be
committed to specific belief in Faunus (to whom, in any case, he gives Greek
poetic features) when he seizes imaginatively on this religious element and
gives it indirect expression in his poetry.

19

Quantum distet ab Inacho
Codrus pro patria non timidus mori
   narras et genus Aeaci
et pugnata sacro bella sub Ilio:

   quo Chium pretio cadum   5
mercemur, quis aquam temperet ignibus,
   quo praebente domum et quota
Paelignis caream frigoribus, taces.

   da lunae propere novae,
da noctis mediae, da, puer, auguris   10
   Murenae: tribus aut novem
miscentur cyathis pocula commodis;

   qui Musas amat imparis,
ternos ter cyathos attonitus petet
   vates: tris prohibet supra   15
rixarum metuens tangere Gratia

   nudis iuncta sororibus.
insanire iuvat: cur Berecyntiae
   cessant flamina tibiae?
cur pendet tacita fistula cum lyra?   20

parcentis ego dexteras
odi: sparge rosas: audiat invidus
    dementem strepitum Lycus
et vicina seni non habilis Lyco.

    spissa te nitidum coma,   25
puro te similem, Telephe, Vespero
    tempestiva petit Rhode:
me lentus Glycerae torret amor meae.

'How far distant from Inachus is Codrus who was not afraid to die
for his country, you keep on telling me, and about the family of
Aeacus and the wars that were fought below sacred Troy: what
price we must pay for a cask of Chian wine (5), who is to heat the
water with fire, who is to provide the house and at what hour
I may rid myself of Paelignian cold, (of all this) you say not a word.

'Quickly pour in honour of the new moon, pour in honour of
midnight, pour, slave, in honour of the augur (10) Murena: drinks
are mixed with three or nine good ladles (of wine). He who loves
the odd-numbered Muses, a bard inspired, he shall ask for thrice
three ladles (15); the Grace, linked with her naked sisters, fearful
of quarrelling, forbids a man to touch more than three.

'I am in the mood to feel inspired: why are the blasts of the
Phrygian pipe not heard? Why is the flute hanging (on the wall)
along with the silent lyre? (20) I abominate stingy right-hands:
scatter roses about. Let Lycus hear our mad noise and envy it:
and let the lady next door, ill matched with old Lycus, hear us (24).

'You are well groomed with your thick hair, you, Telephus,
are like to the unclouded Evening Star, and Rhode, a perfect match,
is looking for you: slow love for my Glycera is burning in me.'

The poet is annoyed: his friend keeps up a tedious discourse on one of the
most technically difficult subjects in the ancient world—the chronological
relationship between one another of the different dating-systems of different
states. Inachus was the first king of Argos and Codrus (who disguised him-
self so that invading Dorians could not avoid killing him and so broke a
solemn injunction) was the last on the Athenian king-list. The boring fellow
also insists on sorting out the fantasticany intricate family-tree of the house
of Aeacus (to which Achilles belonged), and his interest in Troy is not heroic

but only in the relationship between the various wars fought there. Now (5–8) the poet pours out a seemingly endless stream of questions, all subjunctive and therefore dependent on the long-postponed verb *taces* (8). This stanza contains important clues to the poem's setting. The poet wants to know what he must pay for a bottle of one of the best Greek wines (Chian), who is providing hot water (to dilute the wine—and this was an Italian luxury rather than Greek),[1] who is providing the house, and at what time may the poet escape from Paelignian cold (i.e. when does the party start?). The questions point unmistakably to a characteristically Greek situation, which is clear, for instance, in Terence, *Eunuchus* 539 ff.: there a number of young men on guard duty at the Peiraeus agreed to hold a party and put Chaerea in charge of the arrangements; unfortunately Chaerea fell in love with a girl, followed her home, and has just raped her. A companion catches sight of him and is worried that he has done nothing about the party; but all is well and Chaerea has been very efficient. The party is an ἔρανος or bottle-party, where all the guests bring a contribution. In this ode, the bore is in the position of Chaerea and that is why the poet is impatient and why he asks the series of questions. There is no indication to the reader who is providing a house or where; the word *Paelignis* probably does not indicate a venue but is used because the Abruzzi region was proverbial for cold. But the cold is another clue to the reader: the action takes place in midwinter.

But in the very next line the poet is giving a series of orders about toasts and the mixture of wine. The orders create a familiar situation: the poet has constituted himself *arbiter bibendi* and the party has already begun. If so, the reader must understand a considerable gap in time between lines 8 and 9; this is reminiscent of ode 8 where the poet is talking to Maecenas in 1–12, telling him of a party, but in 13 the party has begun and the poet is *arbiter bibendi*. The toasts (for the genitives see on 8. 13) are to the new moon, midnight, and the augur Murena: this man was L. Licinius Varro Murena, brother-in-law of Maecenas and consul in 23 B.C. (though he was probably not the conspirator, executed in 22 B.C., as is usually stated),[2] and he has just been co-opted to the college of augurs (a very high social distinction, rather than one of religious significance). Since the time is midwinter the point of the three toasts is probably that the party is being held on 31 December and the time is midnight (i.e. Murena's tenure of his new

---

[1] The word for the heater used to provide such hot water—*authepsa*— is not attested in Greek literature, but examples of the cooker itself have been recovered from Pompeii (see A. Mau, *Pompeji in Leben und Kunst* [1908], 398–9). The word is Greek but is probably derived from the luxurious civilization of Greek south Italy.

[2] His identity is discussed by K. M. T. Atkinson, *Historia*, 9 (1960), 469 ff.

honour has just commenced). A slave (*puer*) has been ordered to pour these toasts, but the poet continues with a general announcement: the effect of this is that wine is to be mixed in two strengths (either three or nine measures to a given bulk of water). Poets (inspired by the nine Muses) may take (the future *petet* is a polite command) the stronger mixture; but ordinary men, who can only claim the jurisdiction of the three Graces (i.e. witty conversation is their suit), are only permitted by their patron goddesses the weaker mixture. This is, of course, an amusing and self-interested regulation: poetry and Bacchus, wine and inspiration (*attonitus*) were closely connected ideas,[1] and this enables Horace to order for himself, with propriety, more wine than for his companions.

Now (18 ff.) a still later stage of the party arrives as the poet notices the absence of music (the instruments—20—are hanging on the wall) and desires to give rein to the inspiration (*insanire*) which the wine has brought him. This mention of music implies that there are girls present to play it. He condemns thrift (21) and orders roses to be scattered in profusion (a great luxury in winter, brought, for instance, from the famous rose-gardens of Paestum). As the noise increases (*dementem strepitum*), he thinks of the neighbours—and particularly of a neighbour's young wife. With the reflection—that comes easily now—that the young woman is unsuited to her old husband, his thoughts turn directly to love. He pays Telephus (who is probably the bore to whom he was talking at the beginning of the poem) compliments on his beauty and says that Rhode, who is just the right age for Telephus, is eager for him; but the poet is on fire with love for Glycera—and the way he says that indicates a long-felt passion (especially in the word *lentus*). So the poem comes in a circle to end with words to Telephus as it had begun,[2] and also, with the last stanza, the party has moved through its full course towards a climax which is delicately hinted at (compare the end of 28). The reader is probably to understand that the girls mentioned are present—at any rate the present tense *petit* suggests that Rhode is actually making eyes at the handsome Telephus. This casually aroused love in the case of Telephus is contrasted with the poet's resignation to a long predestined passion—in *Odes* i. 19 he falls in love again with Glycera after all was over between them.

The poem is a remarkable example of the way in which Horace uses a traditional form. This is one of many poems which are constructed round the idea of a drinking-party. But it is entirely original, for Horace has presented the whole occasion, right from a time before the party to its

---

[1] See p. 50 above, n. 4, and ode 25.
[2] On this structure, see *Style* F 1.

climax, in a dramatic form that explains nothing outright, but requires the reader to pick out clues and construct the complex and changing occasion for himself.[1] The whole setting is Greek in spirit and expression and names—except for the mention of the Paeligni and the augurship of Murena, set right in the centre of the poem. It is a work of the imagination set in a world of the imagination, but it also gives expression to a closely realized occasion, the drama and human interest of which has a value of its own quite independently of the compliment to Murena.

20

Non vides quanto moveas periclo,
Pyrrhe, Gaetulae catulos leaenae?
dura post paulo fugies inaudax
    proelia raptor,

cum per obstantis iuvenum catervas   5
ibit insignem repetens Nearchum,
grande certamen, tibi praeda cedat
    maior an illa.

interim, dum tu celeris sagittas
promis, haec dentis acuit timendos,   10
arbiter pugnae posuisse nudo
    sub pede palmam

fertur et leni recreare vento
sparsum odoratis umerum capillis,
qualis aut Nireus fuit aut aquosa   15
    raptus ab Ida.

'Do you not see at what peril, Pyrrhus, you stir the cubs of a Gaetulian lioness? In a short while you will run away from the stern contest, a cowardly rapist, when, through the crowds of young men in her path (5), she will come looking for her pretty Nearchus,

---

[1] On this feature, see *Style* D 1.

a mighty contest (to settle) whether the booty falls to you or she is the stronger.

'Meanwhile, as you are bringing out swift arrows and she is sharpening her terrifying teeth (10), the umpire of the contest is said to have put the palm under his bare foot and, in the gentle breeze to be refreshing his shoulders covered with his scented hair (14), as beautiful as either Nireus was or he who was carried off from watery Ida.'

The poet addresses Pyrrhus urgently: he is in great danger, interfering with the cubs of a Nubian lioness. It is a dramatic opening which gives the reader no hint of its real meaning—even the generalizing plural *catulos* (perhaps taken from Homer's simile in *Iliad* xviii. 319) conceals the poet's drift. Nor do the next words help, as the poet foresees that Pyrrhus will fly from the unequal contest, 'a spineless rapist' (a nice oxymoron combines the frightening word *raptor* with the perfect understatement of *inaudax*).[1] The situation is still unclear in line 5, for the 'bands of young men that bar her path' could be hunters, but it is suddenly clear in 6 that it is a beautiful boy who is the object of so many desires of men as well as of the woman described as a 'lioness'. She regards Nearchus as her 'cub' and will search for him if stolen from her—a great contest that will be; the poet drops the phrase *grande certamen* (as an accusative in apposition to the whole sentence) with high melodrama into the picture of the 'lioness's' relentless search. The contest will decide whether Pyrrhus keeps Nearchus or the 'lioness' proves stronger (in 8 *maior an illa*—'or she is the stronger'—is the correct reading, for *maior an illi* could only suggest that the prize was other than Nearchus);[2] the way this is put shows that the 'lioness' is regarded as the owner of Nearchus. Now (9 ff.) the preparations for battle are described on both sides, but in parallel clauses subordinated to *dum* (to be understood also with *haec dentis acuit timendos*), and the poet's attention is totally concentrated on the behaviour of Nearchus. The poet now sees him as the umpire of the fight (*arbiter pugnae*), but he has thrown the palm (to be awarded to the winner) negligently on the ground, and carelessly stands on it, totally absorbed in himself and his beauty. As well he might, for he is as beautiful as Nireus (second only to Achilles in the Greek army before Troy) or Ganymede.

This poem may seem quite artificial at first sight—a 'literary exercise'. It is true that it is homosexual in subject-matter and has its closest analogies

---

[1] This word is probably a Horatian invention for the purpose of the oxymoron, see p. 60 above, n. 2.

[2] Here, even more clearly than in 5. 15 (see p. 55 above, n. 1), the manuscripts are united in giving the incorrect reading *illi*.

in a long series of Greek epigrams about homosexual situations. But Horace has—as often—elevated the epigrammatic material into a poetic form of greater range.[1] He leads only gradually into the situation, and then builds it up swiftly into a heroic confrontation (5–8). Then he seems to maintain this tone as the combatants prepare, but instantly this tone is abandoned for a perfect representation of the total indifference of the cause of the contest to everything except himself. This neat twist stands all the previous solemnity on its head, and the poem slips into a quiet timeless ending that dwarfs all human passions with the perfectly devised recollection of Nireus so long ago and of him who was snatched from many-fountained Ida (*aquosa* aptly recalls the ornamental Homeric adjective πολυπῑ́δαξ). How absurd are human passions—the epigram could not be better done—even the gods fell to the temptation of Ganymede (and were *raptores*— cf. 4).[2]

21

O nata mecum consule Manlio,
seu tu querelas sive geris iocos
    seu rixam et insanos amores
        seu facilem, pia testa, somnum,

quocumque lectum nomine Massicum   5
servas, moveri digna bono die,
    descende, Corvino iubente
        promere languidiora vina.

non ille, quamquam Socraticis madet
sermonibus, te negleget horridus: 10
    narratur et prisci Catonis
        saepe mero caluisse virtus.

tu lene tormentum ingenio admoves
plerumque duro; tu sapientium
    curas et arcanum iocoso   15
        consilium retegis Lyaeo;

---

[1] For this characteristic, see *Style* F III.   [2] See *Style* F I.

tu spem reducis mentibus anxiis,
virisque et addis cornua pauperi
   post te neque iratos trementi
     regum apices neque militum arma.   20

te Liber et, si laeta aderit, Venus
segnesque nodum solvere Gratiae
   vivaeque producent lucernae,
     dum rediens fugat astra Phoebus.

'O born with me when Manlius was consul, whether you bring complainings or jokes or quarrelling and passionate love or, dutiful wine-bottle, gentle sleep, on whatever account you preserve the choice Massic vintage (5), worthy to be served on a high day, come down, since Corvinus bids me bring out rather mellow wines.

'He, although he is soaked in ethical treatises, shall not ignore you boorishly (10): even the virtue of ancient Cato is said often to have been heated up with wine.

'You apply gentle torture to a spirit usually resistant: you reveal the worries of wise men and their secret thoughts with (the help of) the humorous Wine-God (16): you return hope to anxious hearts, and give both strength and horns to the poor man who, after you, trembles neither before the angry crowns of kings nor before the weapons of the soldiery (20).

'Bacchus and, if she will kindly be present, Venus and the Graces, reluctant to loose the knot (that binds them), and the living candles shall lead you on till Phoebus returning puts the stars to flight.'

The initial *o* indicates emotional intensity[1] and it soon becomes clear that the poem is in prayer-form. The vocative *pia testa* is postponed and a descriptive phrase opens the poem. This phrase takes the place of the birth-legend of the deity, which was normally mentioned early in prayers. The deity here addressed was born in the same year as the poet, when L. Manlius Torquatus was consul, in 65 B.C. The postponement of the vocative achieves an element of surprise, since the reader has realized that the poet is praying before he discovers that it is to a bottle of wine (it is *pia* because it faithfully serves the Wine-God).[2] The vocative is set in the last of a series of clauses,

---

[1] See odes 13. 1 and 14. 1.

[2] The relationship of the wine-bottle is complex: on the one hand, to the poet it is a god (so addressed in prayer-form); on the other, it is a servant to the real gods and so, from that point of view, *pia*.

linked by anaphora (*seu . . . sive . . . seu . . . seu . . .*), which culminate in a generalizing phrase (5–6). This phrase is of a familiar pattern: a worshipper, Greek or Roman, had to be certain that he was addressing the intended deity by the correct name (deities tend to have many names and, certainly, different names in different places), but, since he could not easily be certain, he would list all the names he knew and then add an escape-clause such as 'or if there is any other name by which you wish to be called'. Since there could be no doubt about the name of the excellent Massic vintage which Horace addresses, he substitutes speculation about the effect which the wine may produce—complaints, jokes, quarrels, love, or sleep—and so the escape-clause is accommodated to this special purpose: *quocumque nomine* therefore means not, as usual, 'by whatever name' but 'on whatever account' or 'for whatever purpose' (*nomen* having the sense of 'heading'—as in a ledger). The religious ideas are continued in *moveri* (ritual objects were 'moved' in certain cult ceremonies) and *bono die* (a day of good omen); while *descende* is a pleasant piece of blasphemy, for deities are naturally above (see 4. 1) and so are wine-bottles (because they were stored up in the roof).[1] The purpose of the prayer is now made clear (7–8): Horace is entertaining the distinguished M. Valerius Messalla Corvinus. He now hastens to assure the wine-bottle that, in spite of a reputation for 'being soaked' (a pun) in ethical philosophy (this is the main sense of 'Socratic dialogues'), Messalla will not neglect[2] to do honour to it; the poet bolsters his assurance by a deliberately scandalous statement about the ancient M. Cato who was censor in 184 B.C., a man notorious for his righteousness.

The second half of the ode (13–24) consists of praises of the deity in a series of clauses with anaphora:[3] *tu. . . tu . . . tu . . . post te . . . te . . .* The first two clauses (13–16) praise the power of wine to break down the resistance of wise men and make them reveal their secrets (including the worries which—by definition—they should not have). The second two (17–20) move out to express a general power over the human race, and this is made concrete in a striking political scene, quite alien to Rome, of the poor quaking before kings and their bodyguard;[4] this detail opens out the vision to the

---

[1] See ode 8. 10–11 and commentary.

[2] The manuscripts are equally divided as between *neglegit* and *negleget*. Decision here is simple: since the poet is addressing a specific bottle of Massic wine a present tense, stating generally that Messalla does not ignore it, would have no sense addressed to this particular bottle (*te*) which can only be honoured (and drunk) once. An assurance that, if the bottle will kindly descend, Messalla will not ignore it, is perfectly in place.

[3] Compare ode 13. 9 ff. and commentary.

[4] The same political situation, equally briefly depicted, is to be found in odes 1. 5–8, 3. 3, and 16. 9.

Hellenistic kingdoms of the Near East. The final stanza looks as if it, too, praises the power of wine, but, as in 13. 13–16, the tenses change to future. A series of divine creatures is mentioned: Bacchus, Venus (*laeta* is a further religious touch)—and, as if they are of the same company, 'living candles'; they will 'prolong' the bottle of wine, and the verb *producent*, in this context, suggests honour done to the bottle. The candles, appearing with the divine creatures, show that these deities serve a double function. In the hymnic context they do honour to the wine-bottle in their own right. But the poet has also organized his prayer so that it functions as the preparation for a drinking-party. So the deities also serve as symbols of the delights of such a party: Bacchus of the drinking, Venus of the love-making, and the Graces of the pleasures of witty conversation. It is in this aspect of their function that the candles can join them; for, naturally, a pleasant party will continue through the night till dawn.[1] This final stanza, therefore, serves to tie together the two aspects of the poem—the prayer and the preparations made for a drinking-party.

22

Montium custos nemorumque, virgo,
quae laborantis utero puellas
ter vocata audis adimisque leto,
      diva triformis,

imminens villae tua pinus esto,   5
quam per exactos ego laetus annos
verris obliquum meditantis ictum
      sanguine donem.

'Guardian of the mountains and of the groves, Virgin, who, thrice-called, hear girls labouring in childbirth and save them from death, three-formed goddess, let the pine which hangs over my farmhouse be yours (5), so that gladly at the completion of each year I may present it with the blood of a young boar that is still practising its sidelong slash.'

This little poem corresponds to a type of which there is a whole book in the *Palatine Anthology*: the general purpose of these epigrams is to dedicate

[1] See commentary on 8. 14–15.

something to a god.[1] But normally the epigram is written in such a way that it would make sense to inscribe it beside the object. Horace's poem is more complex. The first stanza is an elaborate address to the goddess Diana in which the poet picks out two of her functions for mention: she is goddess of the countryside and also the goddess of childbirth. In this address (1–3) the poet picks one function which she shared with her Greek counterpart, Artemis; but her function as goddess of childbirth was Greek (Artemis Eileithyia, whereas the Romans had Juno Lucina) and, although this function was assimilated poetically to the Roman Diana, the implication cannot be escaped here that as, in 18. 1, Horace viewed Faunus for a moment as Pan, here he views Diana as Artemis, and writes as a poet who is as much at home in the Greek tradition as in the Roman. He does not mention any other function of the goddess, but sums up her complex character in the address *diva triformis* (Luna in the sky, Diana on earth, and Hecate in the underworld— hence Diana of the Crossways or Trivia because her three-formed statue could appropriately be placed where one road merged into another). Now (5) the poet decrees the dedication but, from the way in which he does this, it becomes clear that he is not thinking in terms of a poem to be inscribed near the object (for then he would have said 'this pine'); he is addressing the goddess, but writing a poem to be read. This point becomes clearer in the way in which he promises yearly sacrifice: 'so that I may present it gladly each year with . . .'. The poet is actually speaking to the goddess. The detail of the sacrifice, whereby the young boar comes alive in the vivid and pathetic picture of it practising the mode of attack that it will never grow old enough to use in earnest, recalls the young goat in ode 13. Here, even more than in ode 13, the poet's language recalls the way in which hunters in Greek epigrams dedicate wild animals to Artemis—and the detail here suggests a wild animal. But no hunter would so tempt fortune as to guarantee a certain type of kill, yearly, on a specified day (the phrase *per exactos . . . annos* amounts to a specification of the day). So it is clear that Horace is thinking in terms appropriate to the calculated sacrifice of a domestic pig, but he achieves a moment of pathos and telling detail by describing the animal in terms of a wild creature—which is, of course, appropriate for Diana, the huntress goddess. In this accumulation of detail and range of tone, as well as in the elaborate address to Diana, the poem becomes more complex and subtle than the normal type of Greek dedicatory epigram.[2] It was probably with this intention in mind that the poet chose to stress two very different aspects of Diana and from two cultures. With

---

[1] See Appendix, no. 8.
[2] For this upgrading of the epigram into a major poetic form, see *Style* F III.

this goes the dedication of a tree, which is a typically Italian act (trees decked with garlands appear often in Campanian wall-paintings), and this gives the poet the opportunity for a deft sketch of its relationship to his farmhouse (*imminens villae*...). Finally the pathetic detail of the young boar takes the reader out again into the wild territory of Diana.

23

Caelo supinas si tuleris manus
nascente Luna, rustica Phidyle,
   si ture placaris et horna
      fruge Lares avidaque porca,

nec pestilentem sentiet Africum   5
fecunda vitis nec sterilem seges
   robiginem aut dulces alumni
      pomifero grave tempus anno.

nam quae nivali pascitur Algido
devota quercus inter et ilices   10
   aut crescit Albanis in herbis
      victima pontificum securis

cervice tinget: te nihil attinet
temptare multa caede bidentium
   parvos coronantem marino   15
      rore deos fragilique myrto.

immunis aram si tetigit manus,
non sumptuosa blandior hostia,
   mollivit aversos Penatis
      farre pio et saliente mica.   20

'If you once lift your hands upturned to heaven at the time the new moon is born, Phidyle, dweller in the country, if you placate the Lares with incense and this year's corn and a greedy pig, then neither shall the fruitful vine feel the pestilence of the sirocco (5) nor the corn the sterilizing mildew nor the sweet nurslings the sickly climate in the apple season. For the consecrated victim that pastures over snowy Algidus amidst the oaks and holm-oaks (10), or grows up in Alban meadows, shall stain with his neck the axes of the pontifices: it is no business of yours to approach with great slaughter of sheep the tiny gods that you decorate with rosemary and fragile myrtle (16). Whenever a hand has touched an altar without a gift, though not winning more favour by means of a costly sacrifice, it has (always) appeased the Penates from their wrath with a dutiful (offering of) meal and crackling salt.'

The poet addresses a countrywoman called Phidyle (a significant Greek name from φείδεσθαι and implying thrift), and tells her that if she prays and sacrifices to the Lares at the new moon (i.e. the beginning of the month), then the crops and stock will not suffer harm. The ancients prayed, holding out their hands, palm upwards (*supinas*), towards the sky, after sacrifice. Here the sacrifice is offered to the Lares, the private gods of the household whose images stood in a niche over the hearth; the first day of the new month was a usual time to honour them (Propertius iv. 3. 53). The prayer is to be for the blessings which the poet declares will proceed from such prayer and sacrifice: the vines will take no harm from the sirocco, nor the corn from mildew, nor the young animals from the autumn heat (*annus* with an adjective can mean that part of the year designated by the adjective —so *hibernus annus* means 'the winter season'). It is not clear that the poet is speaking at an identifiable time of the year, but, since *horna fruge* means 'this year's corn', he is probably thinking of a time not later than spring (the ceremony of the Robigalia was held on 25 April).

The poet's thoughts now turn to one of those scenes which he often evokes with deep pleasure: it is in the Alban hills; there is snow on Algidus, one of their highest peaks, and the poet visualizes a victim pasturing in the great area of woods and grassland reserved for the state religion; the victim (*victima* was a large animal—ox, sheep, or sow—while *hostia* was small or young) is destined to meet its end staining the sacrificial axes of the *pontifices*. This picture, vivid with colour, is instantly followed by a contrasting *te*: the poet tells Phidyle that such sacrifice is of no concern to her—she should decorate (the participle *coronantem* describes—and so by implication prescribes—her customary action) the tiny household gods with fragrant flowers. In the final stanza (17–20) the poet goes beyond this concept of appropriate sacrifice to state a more general truth: if a hand touches the altar without an animal to sacrifice, but only the salt and corn which was thrown over the victim, it still never fails to appease (this is the force of the perfect tense *mollivit*) the hostility of the household gods (the word Penates here is applied to them, but, though these were strictly the gods of the store-rooms of the house, Horace intends no distinction). The last words picture the simple act of throwing the meal and salt on the fire, with the vivid detail of the salt sparkling.

The interest of the theme of sacrifice to the poet lies here in the evocation of a simple rustic piety, an ideal sense of the unchanging values of rural life and its natural relationship with unseen powers. Interpretation of this poem should start with Cato's definition in *de agricultura* 143 of the duties of the *vilica*—the *vilicus* or bailiff supervised work on the farm and stock, the *vilica* correspondingly had her duties in the farmhouse. Among other pro-visions, Cato lays it down that she must not engage in sacrifice herself, or let others do it, without the orders of her master or mistress: she must remember that her master does sacrifice on behalf of the whole household. Later he says that when a holy day coincides with the first day of the month (i.e. the Kalends—and he adds also the Ides and Nones), she must put a garland (*corona*) over the hearth and pray to the household gods. Now Horace seems to have imagined himself into this situation for the purpose of the ode. He addresses Phidyle—a very suitable name for the *vilica*, though Greek according to the lyric convention—as her master (*dominus*) and gently gives her directions for sacrifice to the Lares (for which, accord-ing to Cato, she would need his permission), and, instead of prescribing her prayer, he gives its content in the form of a prediction (5–8). From this simple ceremony his thought ranges out by contrast to the great state sacrifices, and then right back beyond the sacrifice for which he has given permission to the usual religious observation of Phidyle; this is, exactly as Cato describes it, the dedicating of a fragrant garland to the Lares (15–16). Finally, to bring out the inner value of a religious act as a state of mind and an intention rather than as a gift to be assessed simply in cash terms, he visualizes the sacrifice, which he authorized at the beginning, being carried out without its main element, the animal. But there is a danger of attributing a Christian spirituality to these words. The poet has treated the *far et sal* as if it were not a real gift (*immunis*) for two reasons: first, at sacrifice the victim was sprinkled with meal and salt, so the *far et sal* stands for the absence of a real sacrifice; secondly, an offering of *far et sal* to the Penates was a normal act accompanying a meal (see Fowler, *Religious Experience of the Roman People*, 73). The poet makes it clear that a sacrifice would be a more acceptable offering (*blandior*); yet, if that is not possible, the Penates can be mollified (i.e. they will not express anger) by *far et sal*. There is a narrow path to be walked here between Christian emphasis on the state of mind or intention of the worshipper and a crude commercial assessment of the value of a sacrifice; Roman religion, a formalized and traditional pattern of behaviour, tended to the latter view but did not exclude something of the former. Piety for Romans was not just the performance of due rites at prescribed times. But the poet's intention will be totally distorted if this ode is read as a sort of sermon on religious observance; this poem is another expression of his love for the simple, quiet life, especially where the traditions of centuries were being maintained by the natural piety of a rural community.

24

Intactis opulentior
thesauris Arabum et divitis Indiae
    caementis licet occupes
terrenum omne tuis et mare publicum,

    si figit adamantinos   5
summis verticibus dira Necessitas
    clavos, non animum metu,
non mortis laqueis expedies caput.

    campestres melius Scythae,
quorum plaustra vagas rite trahunt domos,   10
    vivunt et rigidi Getae,
immetata quibus iugera liberas

    fruges et Cererem ferunt,
nec cultura placet longior annua,
    defunctumque laboribus   15
aequali recreat sorte vicarius.

    illic matre carentibus
privignis mulier temperat innocens,
    nec dotata regit virum
coniunx nec nitido fidit adultero;   20

    dos est magna parentium
virtus et metuens alterius viri
    certo foedere castitas;
et peccare nefas aut pretium est mori.

    o quisquis volet impias   25
caedis et rabiem tollere civicam,
    si quaeret PATER URBIUM
subscribi statuis, indomitam audeat

    refrenare licentiam,
clarus postgenitis: quatenus—heu nefas!—   30
    virtutem incolumem odimus,
sublatam ex oculis quaerimus invidi.

    quid tristes querimoniae,
si non supplicio culpa reciditur,
    quid leges sine moribus   35
vanae proficiunt, si neque fervidis

    pars inclusa caloribus
mundi nec Boreae finitimum latus
    durataeque solo nives
mercatorem abigunt, horrida callidi   40

    vincunt aequora navitae,
magnum pauperies opprobrium iubet
    quidvis et facere et pati
virtutisque viam deserit arduae?

    vel nos in Capitolium,   45
quo clamor vocat et turba faventium,
    vel nos in mare proximum
gemmas et lapides, aurum et inutile,

summi materiem mali,
mittamus, scelerum si bene paenitet.   50
    eradenda cupidinis
pravi sunt elementa et tenerae nimis

    mentes asperioribus
formandae studiis. nescit equo rudis
    haerere ingenuus puer   55
venarique timet, ludere doctior

seu Graeco iubeas trocho
seu malis vetita legibus alea,
    cum periura patris fides
consortem socium fallat et hospites,   60

    indignoque pecuniam
heredi properet. scilicet improbae
    crescunt divitiae: tamen
curtae nescio quid semper abest rei.

Although, richer than the unrifled treasuries of the Arabs and of
wealthy India, you invest with your building materials the whole of
the land and the sea which is public property (4), if terrible Necessity
drives her adamantine nails into the top of your roof, you shall not
free your mind from fear nor your head from the nets of death (8).

'The Scythians of the plains live better, whose wagons after their
custom draw their vagrant homes (10), and the stern Getae, for
whom unmeasured acres produce free crops and corn; and cultiva-
tion that lasts longer than a year is not their way, but a successor
relieves the man who has completed his period of work with an
equal allotment of labour (16). There, the innocent stepmother is
kind to her step-children, deprived of their own mother, and no
dowried wife lords it over her husband or puts her trust in a smart
adulterer (20). Virtue is the great dowry of their parents and chastity
that with inviolable bond shuns a second man; to sin against this is
forbidden or the penalty is death (24).

'O whoever shall wish to put an end to impious slaughter and
civic savagery, if he shall seek to be inscribed on statues as the patron

of cities, let him be brave to rein in uncontrolled licentiousness (29)—a famous man in the eyes of later generation, since (how wrong it is!) we belittle virtue when it is present amongst us, yet, hard to please, search for it when it is taken from us (32).

'What is the point of sad lamentations if sin is not pruned by punishment (34), or of laws that are useless without morality, seeing that neither the part of the world that is fenced about with fierce heat nor the region that borders on the Arctic nor snows packed hard on the earth deter the merchant (40), while sailors overcome stormy waters by their skill, and poverty, a great disgrace, makes men both do and put up with anything and desert the hard road of virtue (44)?

'If we are truly penitent of our crimes let us deposit our gems and precious stones and our useless gold, the root of the worst evils, either in the Capitol where the shouting and crowd of those who agree encourage us or else into the nearby sea (50).

'The roots of depraved desires must be eradicated and characters that are too soft must be shaped in sterner pursuits. The freeborn boy does not know, through inexperience, how to stay on a horse (55) and is frightened to hunt, more skilled at playing, if you so bid him, with the Grecian hoop, or, if you prefer it, with the dice forbidden by law, since his father's cheating methods defraud his business partner and guests (60), and are in haste (to make) money for a worthless heir.

'Assuredly, wealth grows insatiably: yet always something is missing and the fortune deficient.'

The poem opens on a note of hyperbole—a man richer than the treasuries of Arabia and India (proverbially wealthy as the origin of precious stones and metals) that lie beyond the reach of Roman hands (*intactis*). The poet invites the reader to imagine himself such a man and then using this vast wealth to cover with his building all the land (*terrenum* is not so much 'land' contrasted with 'sea' as land suited for agriculture and so valuable in itself) and the sea (which is naturally the common property of mankind). The picture is of a rich Roman with a villa built not just on the sea-coast but projecting out into the sea—a fashionable practice at the time. A grim picture follows of Death (*Necessitas*—the inevitability of fate)[1] driving nails of adamant into the roof-top. The picture is suggestive rather than precise: fate is

---

[1] The picture of the rich man ambitiously building is close to that in ode 1. 33-40, and in that ode too Death appeared as *Necessitas* (14).

imagined, as the Etruscans saw her, a builder on her own account; but her buildings, unlike those of men, are unbreakable. The idea of her driving nails into the roof-top suggests the wretched man just completing his own building when Death sets her own finishing touch to it. But there is also a hint of a curious Roman custom which the Romans learnt from Etruria, whereby the *pontifex maximus* drove a nail into a wall at the beginning of a new year to symbolize the completion of the previous one: that is why the poet has armed Death with nails—she marks the end of the man's life. When this happens, says the poet (7–8), terror will overcome you and you will be held fast in Death's net (like a trapped animal).

Now (9–24) the poet's vision moves out to a better way of life: the primitive communism of the nomadic tribes on the steppes of South Russia. They are a far-off, romantic people who share property (so their 'acres' are 'unmeasured'), work, and produce (which is therefore 'free to all'),[1] constantly on the move. So (unlike the rich man) they have no wealth whatever, and enjoy consequent advantages: stepmothers (proverbially unkind to their step-children since they wished their own children to inherit all) are kind to step-children, and, since there are no dowries, there are no henpecked husbands (conventional figures of comedy), but wives are faithful (because subject to their husbands). This last thought has switched the movement of ideas into a new direction. That this is a carefully planned move by the poet is shown by the fact that these primitive communists were famous in the ancient world for carrying their communism to its logical conclusion and having women in common too. So, clearly there could be no talk of faithfulness and chastity, but the poet has deliberately chosen to represent these people as having the highest possible regard for the sanctity of marriage. His intention, therefore, is to establish a close relationship between wealth and immorality and between absence of wealth and morality. He represents the marriage-vow (*certo foedere*) as absolute among these people and the penalty for breaking it as death (*aut pretium est mori*).

A pause, and the poet now (25–32) addresses a category of individuals in emotional terms (*o*); the address is, in fact, to any man who will be willing to put an end to civil war. If such a man shall wish to earn the gratitude and admiration of his fellow citizens (*pater urbium* does not designate any technical title—*pater* is a term of respect like 'patron'—but the title *pater patriae* is in the background), then he must curb immorality—though his fame will only be recognized after his death (30–2). The poet purports to generalize

---

[1] The implication that they are 'free' also in the sense of not costing money comes from an extension of the fact that the land and crops are not subject to ownership.

the address here, and the effect of this is not only to avoid naming an individual but also to suggest that such actions as the poet recommends always meet with severe opposition. There is no doubt that the person intended is Augustus, nor that the poet is also thinking of his strenuous attempts at moral legislation.[1] The advice given by the poet has another effect: it connects the idea of ending civil war and making moral reforms in such a way as to suggest that the latter is essential to the former and that opposition to the latter is opposition also to the former. But the implicit encouragement is strong: posterity will recognize the benefactor. What connects this section of the poem (25–32) to the previous one (9–24) is the concept of morality, as it was the concept of wealth—or its absence—that linked that section to the first (1–8). The poet has now collected his themes together —a complex interlacing of concepts of wealth and morality and civil war —and the rest of the poem works them out in terms of the contemporary situation.

Here the first section (33–44) takes up the idea of opposition to moral reform and asks what good lamentation is without penal legislation (33–4) and what good legislation is anyway without a basic change of heart (35–6). It now becomes clear that the basic change the poet requires is in the attitude to wealth, absence of which (i.e. poverty) men regard as the worst of disgraces, but to make money they dare any danger, undergo any hardship (36–41). The poet's call is to deposit wealth in the Capitol (as Augustus did in 28 B.C.—Suetonius, *Aug.* 30) or throw it in the sea; and he adds, significantly, 'if we are truly repentant of our crimes' (50). In these words he refers, as so often, to civil war, and so he gives a depth to his recommendations by connecting again here (as in 25–6) the idea of civil war with that of wealth: those are themes that go together in this poem, without the poet's feeling it necessary to spell out the connection. The poet's mind now goes to the root, and the idea that children need to be brought up differently: to learn manly Roman pursuits, demanding physical hardihood (such as Augustus was reintroducing),[2] rather than effeminate Greek games of skill and chance (dicing was forbidden from early times by Roman law). But as he says it, the poet thinks of the parent, so intent on profit that he cheats his friend and business-partner (*consortem socium*), and even guests in his home (*hospites*)—breaking the basic unwritten code. And why? Only, after all, to pile up money that an equally no-good (*indigno*) heir will dissipate (61–2). A final, depressing, explanatory thought occurs to the poet, introduced by the slow, ponderous particles *scilicet . . . tamen . . .*

---

[1] See p. 5 above and also ode 6 (with commentary)
[2] See p. 35 above, n. 2.

Men cannot help it: once they get the desire for wealth it feeds on itself and is never satisfied. It is a pessimistic ending that brings the poem round in a circle towards the foreboding picture from which it started.

This poem needs to be set in the political context of 28/27 B.C.: the civil wars have, in fact, been ended by the battle of Actium in 31 B.C.; but no one could be sure of that at the time and what looks like a dangerous crisis has been caused by the failure of Augustus' attempts at moral reform.[1] In these circumstances, the poet's vision is of a deep-rooted malaise in Roman society, and the vision comes to him in a series of contrasting pictures: the rich man's pretentious sea-villa and the horrific Etruscan figure of Death; the romantic nomads and their strange life; the figure of the reformer in history, rejected in his own lifetime; merchants and sailors in danger on the equator[2] and in northern seas; dedications on the Capitol; the pursuits of the young; the hopeless greed of their parents. The connecting thread from beginning to end is the idea that all evils in society stem from the greed for wealth. The conviction often came to the poet—as it came to many men before and since; that is not significant. What matters is that it came to the poet as a vision that imposed a unity on a great series of pictures and impressions in his mind, giving him a new and exciting view of the human scene. The first three sections of the poem (1–32), which set out the complexity of thematic material, are excellent: the poet's vision is fresh and strong and concrete. But the second half of the poem (33–64), in which the themes are applied directly to the contemporary situation, becomes too didactic; the poet is too factually involved in exhorting and recommending and condemning. In the first half of the poem the poet's view was implicit in the pictures, to be sensed by the reader; but in the second half the poet explains and justifies.

25

Quo me, Bacche, rapis tui
plenum? quae nemora aut quos agor in specus
velox mente nova? quibus
antris egregii Caesaris audiar

---

[1] See pp. 4–5 above.

[2] The words (37) *pars inclusa caloribus* express an idea which rested on a curious Greek and Roman geographical misconception. Strabo reports the opinion of Eratosthenes and Polybius that the torrid zone is only so at its northern and southern extremities, and that it encloses a temperate zone which straddles the equator (see A. E. Housman's 'Astronomical Appendix' to his *Lucan*, p. 331).

aeternum meditans decus   5
stellis inserere et consilio Iovis?
    dicam insigne recens adhuc
indictum ore alio. non secus in iugis

exsomnis stupet Euhias
Hebrum prospiciens et nive candidam   10
    Thracen ac pede barbaro
lustratam Rhodopen, ut mihi devio

ripas et vacuum nemus
mirari libet. o Naiadum potens
    Baccharumque valentium   15
proceras manibus vertere fraxinos,

nil parvum aut humili modo,
nil mortale loquar. dulce periculum est,
    o Lenaee, sequi deum
cingentem viridi tempora pampino.   20

'Whither are you whirling me away, Bacchus, filled with you?
Into what groves, into which caves am I being hurried so swiftly,
changed in spirit? In what caverns shall I be heard rehearsing to set
the eternal glory of great Caesar among the stars and in the council
of Juppiter (6)? I shall sing something great, completely new, never
spoken by another's mouth. Not otherwise, out on the mountain-
ridges, is the sleepless Bacchante astonished as she looks over Hebrus
and Thrace white with snow (10) and Rhodope trodden by barbar-
ian feet, than I, in this remote region, am happy to feel inspiration
at river-banks and a deserted grove. O master of the Naiads and of the
Bacchantes strong (15) to uproot tall ash-trees with their hands,
nothing small or in humble style, nothing mortal shall I sing. A sweet
danger it is, o God of the Wine-Press, to follow a divinity who
wreathes his temples with green vine-leaves.'

The poem opens dramatically with the poet in the grip of a mystical ex-
perience, and this sensation is expressed in three excited questions which both
form a tricolon *crescendo* and become more specific. Bacchus is the god

addressed: not only the god of wine, but, as Dionysus, the author and deity of the most violent religious cult known to antiquity. He is well suited to originate a poet's divine frenzy of inspiration. So, first, the poet asks 'where?', feeling himself possessed by the god (*tui plenum* is Latin for ἔνθεος). But then he recognizes groves and caves—traditionally associated with poetic inspiration—so, 'filled with a new spirit' (a variation on *tui plenum*), he asks where are these groves and caves? Then, as there comes with increasing clarity across his mind the outline of his inspiration, he anticipates the composition of a poem and asks 'What caves are these in which I shall compose it?' The questions 'Where?', What groves and caves . . .?', and 'In what caves . . .?' are not so much requests for information (which could be answered by saying 'The cave in such and such a place, etc.') as a means of expressing the bewildering strangeness of the experience. The subject, which he sees more clearly, is political: the great work of Augustus will be done and the poet will see him finding a place (like his adoptive father, Julius Caesar) in the heavens and joining the council of Juppiter—the poet will put him there by representing him in a poem as destined to go there. When the questions finish, the poet is sure and confident: the poem will be totally original. This was something that Bacchus could guarantee his followers, and so, even in the procession of the Phallophori, the participants claimed total originality for the hymn with which they honoured the god (Athenaeus, *Deipnosophistae* xiv. 622 c). And it is to a precise analogy from Dionysiac rites that the poet's thoughts now turn (8 ff.) as a wonderfully evocative picture comes to him of the Bacchante (called Euhias from her ritual cry of *euhoe*) on the mountain-ridges at night (this is the sense of *exsomnis*), gazing over the strange landscape laid out before her eyes: the river Hebrus and Thrace white with snow and the great mountain Rhodope, so far north that only the feet of barbarians tread it. It is an arresting vision and conveys with force the strangeness the poet feels as he gazes so unexpectedly on river-banks and lonely groves (places of poetic inspiration). The loneliness, which is so well caught in the picture of Rhodope where only barbarian feet tread, is an essential detail in this mystical experience—it is not a social or gregarious experience. The correlatives with which this comparison is made are themselves strange and without parallel: *non secus . . . ut . . .* (where *ac* would be normal).

The questions (1 ff.) moved from being an address to the god to become increasingly a form of self-expression, leading to the comparison of the poet's experience (8 ff.). Now (14 ff.) the poet returns to the god in a form of prayer. He uses an honorific phrase which recalls the power given by the god to Naiads and Bacchantes; then he does not ask the god, but asserts that his poem will not be minor or mortal. The implication is that, as the god gives unheard-of power to the Bacchantes, so he will to the poet; but the form of expression recalls the way Virgil, for instance, declares his own epic theme while calling on the Muse (cf. especially *Aeneid* vii. 37–44; i. 1–11 is more straightforward). The poet makes explicit the special nature of the god's help in the striking statement that it is a pleasurable danger to follow Bacchus. This omission of the actual request to the god and the final statement are perfectly calculated to suggest a peculiar fact about this god: his inspiration comes not just at the asking for it, but in an inexplicable way and when the worshipper may well not expect it—all the poet can do is to give way and follow.

The poem is subtly constructed: poetic inspiration alternates with its analogue, Dionysiac frenzy (8–12: 12–14; 14–16: 17–18), till the final sentence covers both types of experience and also picks up the theme, with which the poem began, of the god's calling the worshipper to follow. The danger which adds spice, as it were, to the pleasure is clear enough in the case of the Bacchantes: to lose one's senses and become filled with a spirit that manifests itself as frenzy is to lose control of oneself, and Euripides memorably portrayed the result in his *Bacchae*. The danger for the poet is only partly the similar sense of being possessed by another's will. Here comparison with similar themes in other poems can help. Horace several times (e.g. iii. 4. 1–4; iv. 6. 1–28) calls on a god for inspiration, there is a pause, and then the poet feels the inspiration (iii. 4. 5–8 and iv. 6. 29–30) and moves straight into poetical composition. This separates the three elements: the prayer, the inspiration, and the subject. In this ode, however, the poet has tried to give an impression of the way in which in reality the three elements are indistinguishable, totally confused. So the subject has emerged in the course of the inspiration, but the poet has had to express it with more precision than is convincing in the circumstances. This only underlines, however, his desire to make clear that he is not trying to express the sensation of poetical inspiration in general, but the specific inspiration which he felt for poetry on political themes. This type of poetry was virtually an invention of Augustan poets (especially Horace), and here lies the danger which he feels: it is an entirely new field and an extremely tricky subject since the poet, who is no politician, can only treat it to a large extent from outside.

26

Vixi puellis nuper idoneus
et militavi non sine gloria:
   nunc arma defunctumque bello
    barbiton hic paries habebit,

laevum marinae qui Veneris latus   5
custodit. hic, hic ponite lucida
   funalia et vectis et arcus
    oppositis foribus minaces.

o quae beatam diva tenes Cyprum et
Memphin carentem Sithonia nive,   10
   regina, sublimi flagello
    tange Chloen semel arrogantem.

'I have lived my life, till lately popular with girls, and I have
been a soldier not without renown: now these weapons and this
lyre that has completed its military service this wall shall keep
which guards the left side of sea-born Venus (5). Here, here place
the gleaming torches and the crowbars and the bows that threaten
barred doors:
   ' "O goddess, you who dwell in blessed Cyprus and Memphis
that is free from Thracian snow (10), queen touch just once with
uplifted lash Chloe the arrogant".'

The first word sounds a sombre note as if the poet's life were over—as in a
sense it is (so, seriously, Virgil makes Dido say in her last speech on the funeral
pyre *vixi et quem dederat cursum Fortuna peregi*: 'My life is over and the span
that Fate gave me is accomplished'—*Aeneid* iv. 653). But it is the poet's
love-life which is over and he recalls honourable service in love's warfare
(Greek and Roman writers often view love—not without some cause—as a
war and use metaphors taken from that sphere). It becomes clear (4–6) that
the poet is in a temple of Venus, for he points to the left-hand wall and says
that his weapons and lyre (used for serenading) will hang there. In line 6
the imperative *ponite* shows that he has a retinue of slaves loaded with the

tools, as it were, of his trade; these are torches, crowbars, and bows—all weapons for use in assaulting a besieged city or a girl's door barred against the poet. There is, for instance, a famous scene in the *Eunuchus* of Terence where the soldier comes with his followers (some armed with slings) to assault the house of Thais and abstract the girl: such a scene is part of the humorous convention of Greek and Roman erotic poetry. Having given his orders, the poet now (9 ff.)—very properly—commences a prayer to Venus, and the reader expects a prayer of dedication. The prayer is in high solemn style, listing the various dwelling-places of the goddess; this is a traditional feature of prayer and was not only honorific but—like the listing of a god's various names (see on 21. 5–6)—ensured that the worshipper directed his prayer to the right quarter and, as it were, caught the god at home. So Cyprus, Venus's most famous home, is mentioned and then, surprisingly, Memphis, for, though the goddess had a temple there, it was not likely to spring to mind so easily. But Memphis is given a curiously decorative phrase that is rather like saying that Tunis is free from Caledonian mist, for Sithonia was Thrace in the north of Greece, while Memphis was in the hot sands of the upper Nile. But the names are also significant, for the poet is going to mention his girl, Chloe, who came from Thrace (9. 9), and her chilly home no less than her chilly treatment of the poet contrasts amusingly with the goddess's far from chilly home and nature. Here, at the climax of the poem, comes an amusing surprise: the poet, who purports to be retiring and making a dedicatory prayer, asks—of all things—for one more chance with Chloe. What had made the poet go through the elaborate ritual of retirement, the reader suddenly realizes, was Chloe's persistent 'No' to the poet; that is the reason for the sad opening and the picture of a life now over—at least as far as girls are concerned.

There are two types of Greek epigram which lie behind this poem: the one is the straightforward dedication of tools or equipment by a workman or, for example, a fisherman as a token of his retirement and gratitude to the gods for what success he had; the other is the type of dedicatory epigram where the dedicant is not retiring but asking for greater success[1]—he is to be imagined as dedicating, not his actual tools, but pictures or replicas of them. Horace has combined the two to create a poem on a larger scale than epigram and with a wider range of tone,[2] so that, in spite of the sad and solemn panoply of retirement, retirement is the last thing he wants—what he wants is greater success.

[1] See Appendix, nos. 5, 6, and 7.
[2] On this characteristic, see *Style* F III.

27

Impios parrae recinentis omen
ducat et praegnans canis aut ab agro
rava decurrens lupa Lanuvino
    fetaque vulpes,

rumpat et serpens iter institutum
si per obliquum similis sagittae
terruit mannos: ego cui timebo
    providus auspex,

antequam stantis repetat paludes
imbrium divina avis imminentum,   10
oscinem corvum prece suscitabo
    solis ab ortu.

sis licet felix ubicumque mavis,
et memor nostri, Galatea, vivas,
teque nec laevus vetet ire picus   15
    nec vaga cornix.

sed vides quanto trepidet tumultu
pronus Orion? ego quid sit ater
Hadriae novi sinus et quid albus
    peccet Iapyx.   20

hostium uxores puerique caecos
sentiant motus orientis Austri et
aequoris nigri fremitum et trementis
    verbere ripas.

sic et Europe niveum doloso   5
credidit tauro latus et scatentem
beluis pontum mediasque fraudes
    palluit audax.

nuper in pratis studiosa florum et
debitae Nymphis opifex coronae,   30
nocte sublustri nihil astra praeter
    vidit et undas.

quae simul centum tetigit potentem
oppidis Creten, 'pater, o relictum
filiae nomen, pietasque' dixit   35
    'victa furore!

unde quo veni? levis una mors est
virginum culpae. vigilansne ploro
turpe commissum, an vitiis carentem
    ludit imago   40

vana, quae porta fugiens eburna
somnium ducit? meliusne fluctus
ire per longos fuit, an recentis
    carpere flores?

si quis infamem mihi nunc iuvencum   45
dedat iratae, lacerare ferro et
frangere enitar modo multum amati
    cornua monstri.

impudens liqui patrios Penatis,
impudens Orcum moror. o deorum   50
si quis haec audis, utinam inter errem
    nuda leones!

antequam turpis macies decentis
occupet malas teneraeque sucus
defluat praedae, speciosa quaero   55
    pascere tigris.

"vilis Europe", pater urget absens,
"quid mori cessas? potes hac ab orno
pendulum zona bene te secuta
    laedere collum;

sive te rupes et acuta leto
saxa delectant, age te procellae
crede veloci, nisi erile mavis
    carpere pensum

regius sanguis, dominaeque tradi   65
barbarae paelex." ' aderat querenti
perfidum ridens Venus et remisso
    filius arcu.

mox, ubi lusit satis: 'abstineto'
dixit 'irarum calidaeque rixae,   70
cum tibi invisus laceranda reddet
    cornua taurus.

uxor invicti Iovis esse nescis:
mitte singultus, bene ferre magnam
disce fortunam; tua sectus orbis   75
    nomina ducet.'

'May the omen of a hooting owl start impious men (on their journeys) and a pregnant bitch or a tawny she-wolf racing down from the fields of Lanuvium and a vixen with young; and when their journey has begun may a snake break it (5), if, shooting across the road, it has terrified the ponies. For the person on whose behalf I, as an augur who can see the future, shall feel apprehensive, I shall by my prayer call out from the sun's rising an oracular crow before that bird, prophetic of impending rain, can make back to the stagnant marshes (12).

'You may be happy wherever you prefer, and live without forgetting me, Galatea, and neither woodpecker on the left nor vagrant crow may forbid your journey (16). But do you notice how stormily Orion plunges down the sky? I know well what harm the black gulf of the Adriatic is capable of and the cloudless Iapygian wind (20). May the wives and sons of our enemies feel the blind fury of the rising south wind and the roar of black waters and the shores trembling with the blow.

'In just the same way Europe trusted her snow-white body to the treacherous (25) bull and for all her courage grew pale at the sea alive with monsters and at the dangers in its midst. Not long before in meadows seeking flowers and making a garland she had vowed to the Nymphs (30) now in the glimmering night she saw nothing but the stars and the waters. She, as soon as she landed on Crete powerful with its hundred cities, said "Father—o name of daughter abandoned and filial duty (35) overcome by passion! Whence have I come, where have I arrived? One death is a light (penalty) for the sin of virgins. Am I awake as I lament a disgraceful sin or am I free from stain and does a vain imagining (40) delude me which, speeding from the ivory gate, brings a dream? Was it preferable to journey over the long waves or to gather fresh flowers? Should anyone now give me, angry as I am, that infamous bull (46), I should try to gash it with steel and smash the horns of the monster that recently I loved so deeply. Shamelessly I have left the household of my father: shamelessly I am keeping Orcus waiting. O if any of you gods hear this, would that I might stray naked among lions (52); before disfiguring age wastes these pretty cheeks and the juice dries out of a luscious victim, beautiful as I am, I ask to be fed to tigers (56). Worthless Europe, your distant father insists, why hesitate to die? You can break your neck, hanging from this ash-tree by the girdle that is luckily still with you (60). Or if crags and rocks sharp for death delight you, come, trust yourself to the swift breeze; unless you prefer, a king's daughter, to take a slave's allotted task and be handed over, a concubine, to the charge of a barbarian mistress (66)."

'As she moaned, Venus was suddenly there, smiling treacherously, and her son, his bow now unstrung. After a time, when she had enjoyed herself enough, "Cease" she said "from your tantrums and your heated recriminations (70), for the bull you hate will give you his horns to tear. You have no idea how to be the wife of almighty Juppiter. Stop that sobbing; learn to bear high fortune properly: half the world (75) will bear your name."'

The ode opens with a long and impressive sentence that runs from lines 1–12 and is divided into two parts, which concern the wicked (*impios*) and the poet's friends (*ego cui timebo*) respectively: let the wicked have evil omens to start or ruin their journey; the poet will use his skill to arrange good omens for his friends. The detailed elaboration of the omens (owl, pregnant bitch, female wolf on the left, fox with young, snake darting across the path) parody the Roman interest in the highly technical subject of augury; the construction of the sentence changes for the last and most detailed incident, the one best calculated to break the journey altogether. The poet will help his friends by summoning a crow from the east, a lucky quarter, before it has a chance to slip round and appear from the marshes (which would signify rain). This sentence, with its contrasts, seems general, and its particular application only becomes clear in 13 ff. From these words it appears that the poet has already exercised his good offices and obtained a favourable omen, for he assures Galatea of good fortune wherever she prefers (13). He has reserved the girl's name for the important point where he asks her to remember him (14). Each of the clauses which follow *licet* (13) becomes more specific and relevant to the present instant: so the poet finally declares that no thought of ill omen need prevent her journey. But instantly a means of delay occurs to him: Orion is setting, it is November, he has cause to know what the Adriatic can be like and the west wind, even when it is cloudless (17–20). He wishes such experiences on the wives and children of the enemy (an ancient form of prayer whereby one asked the god to divert one's troubles to an enemy)—but it is a sinister wish, and is equivalent to the English phrase: 'I would not wish it on my worst enemy' (21–4). So from helping Galatea's journey, the poet has come round to doing his best to deter her, and now warns her by the example of Europe. The relevance of Europe is only immediate and superficial: Europe started happily enough, but she was not long on the sea before she became frightened and when she got to Crete. . . .

The story of Europe begins at sea, with the monsters and dangers, and the girl is (28) 'bravely frightened'—an oxymoron of a sort that Horace likes.[1] Then he goes back to a time before the bull came to create vividly contrasting scenes: the girl picking flowers to make a garland at a shrine (a modest and maidenly occupation), then the dim night, only the starlight, reflected in the waters, to see (29–32). Only Horace sets the scene at night, but it is an inspired invention for attention is so concentrated on the economy of the scene that the omission of great sections of the story is made immaterial. The highly impressionistic style is continued by moving instantly forward to the landing on Crete (33–4). Here the poet concentrates his whole sense of the strange story in a speech of the girl[2] (34–66). She

[1] Compare *splendide mendax* in ode 11. 35.
[2] For this method of treating a narrative, see p. 83 above, n. 1.

begins to address her father (34), but she has deserted him and allowed the madness of love (*furor*) to overcome filial duty (*pietas*). She is bewildered and the question *unde quo veni?* (37) is not only geographical, but even more 'To what state (i.e. depth of disgrace) have I come?' To die once is insufficient penalty for a maiden's sin. Then she pinches herself: is she awake and regretting a real sin or is she innocent and was it all a dream? She must reject the easy explanation, for she asks what she has gained by crossing the sea instead of picking flowers (42-4); now she would gladly kill the bull if it were present (45-8). By now she has realized what she has done and the rest of her speech is a melodramatic wish for death: she was shameless in leaving her father's house (symbolized by the household gods), she is now shameless in keeping Orcus (the Italian god of the Underworld) waiting (49-50). She wants to wander naked among lions (a greater temptation and easier prey without clothes); before she grows old and unattractive she wants to feed herself to tigers (53-6). The poet is gently mocking his heroine (and poets who treated such situations too pompously) when he represents her as valuing her beauty only as an appetizer to lions and tigers. She hears her far-off father's voice urging suicide and harshly attaching the adjective *vilis* directly to her name: he offers her an attractively expressed choice of suicides. She could hang herself with her girdle that is luckily still with her;[1] or if cliffs and rocks sharp for death (macabre phrase) delight her, she could trust herself to the gusting wind (always a misplaced trust). Her father puts the alternative clearly; he knows why girls run away from home: the man is usually married and they end up as the wife's slave[2] and the husband's mistress (63-6). She knows her father well enough to put his interpretation on her situation.

But suddenly Venus is there and her son Cupid (the cause of the whole trouble), with his bow now unstrung. Venus enjoys the joke—a treacherous (*perfidum*) pleasure since she planned it all—and finally stops laughing: the girl is to cease her anger (she says this looking back to an earlier part of the girl's speech—45-8): the hated bull will let her tear its horns. This is said jokingly; then Venus becomes serious. Her next words can mean either 'You do not know how to be the wife of Juppiter' or 'You do not know that you are the wife of Juppiter'; in the latter case the construction is a Grecism, as is the construction just used by Venus *abstineto irarum* (69-70). Even if she means the former, she does not also mean that Europe herself knows anything precise, but economically combines the information with the

[1] See p. 140, n. 2 below.
[2] The phrase *carpere pensum* means to take a defined measure of wool (weighed out —*pendere*) for the day's weaving, and the activity is servile.

suggestion that the girl needs to learn how to behave—and follows this immediately with two instructions and a final encouragement (74–6). For this reason—because it is less obvious and more complex—the former meaning is probably correct: Venus is portrayed as enjoying her irony to the full.

Horace in his *Odes* was writing personal lyric and felt obliged, whatever his subject-matter, to find an autobiographical mode of entry into it. But it would be superficial to conclude that 1–24 of this poem is a mere device to enable the poet to introduce the legend of Europe. The poem starts mysteriously in the world of Roman augury, and Galatea, when she enters, is a mysterious creature: her relation to the poet, the nature of her journey, the ominous tone on which the poet leaves her all contrive to create an atmosphere of mystery. This is an invention which is ingeniously calculated to lead into the equally mysterious legend of Europe. Horace's treatment of this is usually undervalued in favour of the clever but trivial conception of Moschos: the Greek *Europe* is a bright, mannered, cynical composition, amusing in a polished and clever, but shallow, way.[1] Horace keeps the mysteries by his imaginative creation of scene and incident no less than by his reticence. Why did the girl go with the bull at all? The poet had an extraordinary situation here and, in the background, memories of the unnatural passion of Pasiphaë (given most imaginative treatment by Virgil in *Eclogues* vi. 45–60); but this would be unsuitable in an innocent girl and so he just hints in (47–8) *modo multum amati | cornua monstri*. Or, did Europe lose her virginity before making the speech? Commentators strenuously deny this because she made the speech as soon as she landed on Crete (33–4). But the poet has left this stage dark so that such a statement has no factual value—if it had, one would be justified in asking what the bull was doing all this time. The girl certainly speaks in a way that would be natural if she were no longer a virgin, and the contrast with her innocence in 29–32 is emphatic. The poet's device of making her wonder if it was all a dream (38–42)—and a false dream—is very ingenious and suggestive. The lines where she imagines her father's assessment (65–6) are usually dismissed as being her own guess about her future if she is captured by the people of the land. But this is to draw in extraneous concepts that have no place in the poem; all that the lines need suggest is that the girl puts into her father's mouth an assessment of her situation which she herself has no reason to deny[2]—in fact, in view of the large area of her experience which the poet

---

[1] Part of it can be found in Appendix, no. 11.

[2] The ironical remark (59) *zona bene te secuta* does not support the girl's innocence, for the *zona*, it need scarcely be said, was not evidence of virginity but merely of a claim to it, or, rather, of an absence of formal marriage.

has left dark, he could well intend to suggest that she had good reason to accept her father's assessment herself. This would motivate her own will to suicide, and would give more basis to the perfidy (67) which the poet attributes to Venus, for she has, in that case, taken pleasure in leading the girl deliberately to a false view of her predicament. This whole interpretation would further give real meaning to Venus' assertion that the girl is (not 'will be') the wife of Juppiter. It is worth considering, in view of the girl's speculation whether the experiences she thought she had were a dream, if the poet is hinting at an interpretation of the legend which viewed the appearance of Juppiter in the form of a bull as a fantasy of the girl's imagination: something of the sort would give more point to Venus' joke (71–2) about the hated bull giving his horns to be torn by the girl.[1] In that case, the girl became 'the wife of Juppiter' during the time when she seemed to herself to be going off with a curiously attractive bull to Crete. It is noticeable that the poet makes the girl move from her speculation about a dream to anger, and she calls the bull *infamem*: this has point if she hints at behaviour which she regards as disgraceful and disgracing. For the word *infamis* is powerful and had a precise sense to Romans: it meant that a man had so behaved as to suffer a degradation from his status as a citizen, involving loss of rights. This penalty was incurred through conviction for a number of offences, prominent among which was rape of a girl against her will. The atmosphere which the poet creates in the girl's dream suggests an act in which she was not a consciously willing participant. It is worth noting that the interpretation suggested here (including the idea that the appearance of Juppiter as a bull is a part of the girl's fantasy) coheres well with the attitude which Horace constantly displays to the mythical, the legendary, and the supernatural: here, as elsewhere, he introduces an element of rationalizing which, without destroying the traditional features of the basic legend or warping them into a crude 'explanation', yet relieves the poet from the necessity of reproducing legends *simpliciter*, as if he took them at face value.

28

Festo quid potius die
Neptuni faciam? prome reconditum,
Lyde, strenua Caecubum
munitaeque adhibe vim sapientiae.

---

[1] It would better represent the amused contempt of Venus' remarks if 71–2 were printed ' . . . *cum tibi invisus laceranda reddet | "cornua" "taurus"* '.

inclinare meridiem   5
sentis ac, veluti stet volucris dies,
    parcis deripere horreo
cessantem Bibuli consulis amphoram?

nos cantabimus invicem
Neptunum et viridis Nereidum comas;   10
    tu curva recines lyra
Latonam et celeris spicula Cynthiae,

    summo carmine, quae Cnidon
fulgentisque tenet Cycladas et Paphum
    iunctis visit oloribus: 15
dicetur merita Nox quoque nenia.

'What better can I do on the feast-day of Neptune? Stir yourself
Lyde, and bring out the Caecuban that is stored away, and make an
assault on entrenched wisdom (4). Do you notice that the midday
is declining and, as if the swift day were standing still, are you
hesitating to snatch from the wine-store the bottle that is slacking
there (from the time) of the consul Bibulus? We shall both sing turn
about of Neptune and the green locks of the Nereids (10): you shall
sing, to the curved lyre, of Latona and the darts of swift Cynthia,
in your last song, of her who dwells in Cnidos and the gleaming
Cyclades and visits Paphos with her team of swans (15): Night too
shall be praised in a well-merited coda.'

The poem opens with the poet posing a question to himself, much as
Catullus in his first poem asks to whom he should dedicate the book: in
neither case does the question indicate uncertainty, rather in both it provides
an informal opening which takes all the circumstances for granted. So
speculation that Horace is out walking and suddenly finds himself at Lyde's
house or that Lyde is Horace's 'housekeeper' are beside the point. The
question also serves to mark the occasion: it is the Roman festival of
Neptunalia on 23 July. The question, as in Catullus, is the signal for instant
action: so the poet bids Lyde bring out the very special Caecuban vintage.
These orders to Lyde make preparations for a party and Lyde is treated
therefore as the more usual slave (see, e.g., 14. 17 ff.). This is to be inter-
preted rather as a poetic economy of character than an indication of Lyde's

social position—though she is probably not thought of as more than a freedwoman. The poet jokes with Lyde in a series of military phrases: *strenuus* (3) is a soldierly virtue and has a tone like 'at the double'; then she is to use the wine as if it were a battering-ram on the fortified citadel of the poet's wisdom (cf. 21. 13 ff.). Now (5–6) he notices that valuable drinking-time is slipping away: he does not say that the day is declining, but the midday—the precision of this departure from the normal phrase is an amusing sign of the poet's anxiety. Lyde is behaving as if time were standing still (6), and she is slow about fetching the wine that is 'slacking' (*cessantem* —the opposite of *strenuus*) in the *apotheca*; the wine too was bottled in a significant consulship, with a well-omened name for Horace's plans, M. Calpurnius Bibulus, and he, if any, was a *cessans*, for, consul with Caesar in 59 B.C., his contribution to politics was to block his colleague's legislation by observing lightning and other omens.

The poet now reviews the pleasures to come: they will sing turn about of Neptune—this was a type of folk-singing popular in Rome and no doubt appropriate on the Neptunalia which was famous as an occasion for singing. But, that done, Horace will leave the musical entertainment to the expert Lyde who will sing to the accompaniment of (*recines*) her lyre. Her songs have significant subjects: the goddesses Leto and her daughter Diana (in her form as Moon-Goddess) will lead finally to Venus, and over her the poet lingers with anticipatory touches of hymnic form, listing her various dwelling-places (see on 26. 9 ff.) and mentioning her famous swan-chariot. This will be the last song, but with suggestive and humorous delicacy the poet says that Night will be hymned in a well-deserved coda (*nenia* was the cry over the dead, then a final song or the end of a song). The feast-day of Neptune will end with love-making.

29

Tyrrhena regum progenies, tibi
non ante verso lene merum cado
   cum flore, Maecenas, rosarum et
    pressa tuis balanus capillis

iamdudum apud me est: eripe te morae,   5
nec semper udum Tibur et Aefulae
   declive contempleris arvum et
    Telegoni iuga parricidae.

fastidiosam desere copiam et
molem propinquam nubibus arduis;   10
    omitte mirari beatae
        fumum et opes strepitumque Romae:

plerumque gratae divitibus vices
mundaeque parvo sub lare pauperum
    cenae sine aulaeis et ostro   15
        sollicitam explicuere frontem.

iam clarus occultum Andromedae pater
ostendit ignem, iam Procyon furit
    et stella vesani Leonis,
        sole dies referente siccos: 20

iam pastor umbras cum grege languido
rivumque fessus quaerit et horridi
    dumeta Silvani, caretque
        ripa vagis taciturna ventis.

tu civitatem quis deceat status   25
curas et Urbi sollicitus times
    quid Seres et regnata Cyro
        Bactra parent Tanaisque discors:

prudens futuri temporis exitum
caliginosa nocte premit deus,   30
    ridetque si mortalis ultra
        fas trepidat. quod adest memento

componere aequus; cetera fluminis
ritu feruntur, nunc medio alveo
    cum pace delabentis Etruscum   35
        in mare, nunc lapides adesos

stirpesque raptas et pecus et domos
volventis una non sine montium
    clamore vicinaeque silvae,
        cum fera diluvies quietos   40

irritat amnis. ille potens sui
laetusque deget, cui licet in diem
    dixisse 'vixi': cras vel atra
        nube polum Pater occupato

vel sole puro; non tamen irritum,   45
quodcumque retro est, efficiet neque
    diffinget infectumque reddet,
        quod fugiens semel hora vexit.

Fortuna saevo laeta negotio et
ludum insolentem ludere pertinax   50
    transmutat incertos honores,
        nunc mihi, nunc alii benigna:

laudo manentem; si celeris quatit
pennas, resigno quae dedit et mea
    virtute me involvo probamque   55
        pauperiem sine dote quaero.

non est meum, si mugiat Africis
malus procellis, ad miseras preces
    decurrere et votis pacisci
        ne Cypriae Tyriaeque merces   60

addant avaro divitias mari:
tunc me biremis praesidio scaphae
    tutum per Aegaeos tumultus
        aura feret geminusque Pollux.

'Etruscan descendant of kings, for you I have had for a long time ready a mellow wine in a cask not yet broached, along with flowers of roses, Maecenas, and balsam pressed for your hair : stir yourself from hesitation (5), do not for ever just keep looking at well-watered Tibur and the sloping fields of Aefula and the ridges of the parricide Telegonus.

'Abandon a plenty that creates boredom and that pile that rears up to the high clouds (10): stop admiring the smoke and riches and noise of wealthy Rome. Very often change, pleasing to the rich, and simple meals at the small homes of poor men, with no tapestries and purple coverlets (15), have smoothed anxiety from their foreheads.

'Now the shining father of Andromeda is displaying his hidden flame, now Procyon (Canis Minor) is raging and the star of furious Leo, as the sun brings back days of drought (20): now the weary shepherd with his sleepy flock makes for shade and the river and the thickets of rough Silvanus and the silent bank is without a breath of wind.

'You keep worrying about what arrangement will suit our state and you are anxiously fearful for our city (26) as to what the Chinese and Bactria ruled by Cyrus may be planning, and the unsettled (region of) the Don: on purpose god hides the issue of time to come in blackness of night (30), and laughs if a mortal is unduly anxious. Remember to make the best of the present moment with equanimity: the rest is carried along like a river, at one time peacefully flowing down in mid-channel to the Etruscan (35) sea, at another whirling rocks it has eaten away and trees it has uprooted and cattle and houses all together, with a roaring echo from the mountains and nearby wood whenever a fierce flood excites the quiet river(41). That man shall live as his own master and in happiness who can say each day "I have LIVED": tomorrow let the Father fill the sky with a black cloud or clear sunshine, yet he shall not make null whatever belongs to the past nor (46) shall he alter and render undone what once the fleeting hour has carried away.

'Fortune taking pleasure in her cruel job and stubborn at playing her high-handed game (50) changes around her unstable honours, kind now to me, now to another: I praise her while she stays with me; if she shakes her swift wings, I give up what she has awarded me and I wrap my virtue close about me and go courting honest poverty that has no dowry (56).

'It is not my way, should the mast groan under African storms, to take refuge in pitiable prayers and bargain with vows that the merchandise of Cyprus and Tyre (60) should not add wealth to the greedy sea: in those circumstances the breeze and twin Pollux will carry me through Aegean storms safe in the protection of the two-oared lifeboat.'

The poem opens with a high-flown circumlocution, followed, two lines later, by the vocative *Maecenas* which it anticipates: that this is not serious flattery of Maecenas' pride in his ancient Etruscan family is shown by the context—it is playful mock-solemnity. The poet has had everything ready for a drinking-party with Maecenas—wine, roses, and balsam for the hair. The poet has described what he has done (1–5); now, by way of contrast, he views it from Maecenas' side (5–8). The names of towns in the beloved Sabine hill-country are evocative of pleasure and pride, and they balance the high-flown address to Maecenas (especially the periphrasis for Tusculum, founded by Telegonus, Odysseus' son by Circe, who unwittingly killed his father). The poet still keeps his eyes on Maecenas' situation but gives his own view of it (9–12): Rome is rich but also noisy and smoky, and wealth brings revulsion (9 *fastidiosam* means 'that produces *fastidium*'); he should leave it and even his great palace on the Esquiline (it 'approaches the clouds' because it is both huge and on a hilltop). In immediate contrast the poet views what his humble way of life can offer (13–16)—namely the sort of change which, by its simplicity, soothes worry, even without rich food, tapestries on the walls (*aulaeis*), and purple coverlets (*ostro*).

So far the stanzas have been arranged in contrasting pairs, and now a further contrast follows: the first stanza (17–20) pinpoints the time of year as late summer; the poet does not say—what is true—that this is a bad time to be in Rome, but follows it instantly by a stanza (21–4) which describes the healthy peace of the countryside and the comforts which its inhabitants enjoy (Silvanus was Italian god of the countryside, corresponding to Greek Pan).[1]

Now (25–8) the poet imagines Maecenas' state of mind as he worries about theoretical (*quis deceat status*) and practical questions of politics, especially about the trouble-spots on the imperial boundaries. But the poet has put these worries in a remote form: political theory had little interest for Romans, the Chinese were far off, 'Bactria ruled by Cyrus' is a high-flown but very remote way of signifying Parthia, and the Tanais or Don (meaning the

---

[1] Silvanus was an ancient Italic deity, a dweller, as his name implies, in the woods; his powers and functions seem to have been close to those of Faunus (see ode 18).

people of that region) is distracted by civil war. So Maecenas' worries are expressed in the least urgent form possible. This stanza too is followed by a contrasting one (29–32) which states that god has so arranged that man cannot—and should not try to—discern the future. With this idea the poet has come not only to a central topic of the poem, but also to a complex and important idea that needs very careful handling. For, although it is possible to say to men, worried with their own affairs, that worry is useless since the future is unknown, it would be both tactless and silly to say this to a man occupied with worry about the nation: not only the intrinsic importance of such a man's worries needs to be recognized but also their altruism. But this is difficult in the context of ideas which Horace has chosen, since the exhortation to 'eat, drink and be merry . . .' rests normally on grounds of pure self-interest.[1] The poet's transition at this point needs careful watching. In a curiously vague phrase (32–3), he advises Maecenas to make the best of the present, and, without pause, plunges into a great simile introduced by the statement that 'everything else (*cetera*) is carried along like a river . . .'. Here the meaning of *cetera* must be restricted to 'the future' (as it is in Tacitus *Annales* i. 49. 1: *clamor vulnera sanguis palam, causa in occulto: cetera fors regit*), but the real point is that the poet's thoughts are moving over an awkward moment to a view of life that he can exemplify in himself, yet cannot really recommend with conviction to Maecenas. The connection is skilfully lost in the magnificent simile of the Tiber (identified by *Etruscum in mare*) at peace and in destructive flood (33–41). Out of the flood emerges an individual who might well be the poet (but this is not stated yet): he is self-sufficient (exemplifying a Greek Stoic ideal) and happy because he lives (with a capital L—*vixi*) for each day alone and takes no thought for the morrow (41–5). The poet pretty well takes over this character as his own as he says 'let god make tomorrow fine or cloudy' (43–5), for this leads straight into a statement, balancing what the poet said of god's disposition of the future in 29–32, that god cannot alter the past. So the six stanzas 25–48 have seen a very skilful thematic modulation by which the poet moved swiftly from an implied (but gentle) condemnation of Maecenas' altruistic worries to a strong recommendation—disengaged from Maecenas—of the life lived in isolation and for the moment.

The poet now returns to a series of contrasted stanzas (arranged in pairs) as he comes to the expression of his own personal ideal (introduced by the picture of the self-sufficient man). Thus a stanza (49–52) describing the activity of Fortune is followed by one describing the poet's attitude to her. Fortune is solemnly described (this is also the effect of the *figura etymologica*

---

[1] For a similar difficulty in ode 8, see p. 73 above.

in 50 *ludum . . . ludere*). The poet's attitude should not be mistaken for prig-
gishness: when he says that he 'wraps himself in his virtue', he alludes
jokingly to a favourite metaphor of Greek philosophers who liked to describe
Virtue as a cloak, and he goes on to say that he 'seeks the hand of honest
poverty in marriage, without a dowry': she will be constant (*probam*),
unlike Fortune. The poet is not only laughing at Greek philosophers and
their pretentious talk, but at himself too.

A final picture, divided into two contrasting scenes, ends the poem.
The poet imagines himself the captain of a merchantman (and in such cases,
as here, it was quite usual for the captain to own both ship and cargo),
carrying a very valuable cargo; there is a storm, but it is no characteristic
of the poet to bargain with the gods in piteous prayers. There is a pause at
61 *mari*, and a sharply contrasting picture appears—the poet in the little
lifeboat (*scapha*, towed behind the ship), being carried to safety by the
breeze and those guardians of sailors, the twins Castor and Pollux. It is a
bright and amusing contrast, a most unexpected idea, to end the poem:
the poet calmly deserts both ship and valuable cargo, unmoved by the enor-
mity of the loss to his pocket—an excellent illustration of his attitude to
Fortune (54 *resigno quae dedit*).

30

Exegi monumentum aere perennius
regalique situ pyramidum altius,
quod non imber edax, non Aquilo impotens
possit diruere aut innumerabilis

annorum series et fuga temporum.   5
non omnis moriar, multaque pars mei
vitabit Libitinam: usque ego postera
crescam laude recens, dum Capitolium

scandet cum tacita virgine pontifex.
dicar, qua violens obstrepit Aufidus   10
et qua pauper aquae Daunus agrestium
regnavit populorum, ex humili potens

princeps Aeolium carmen ad Italos
deduxisse modos: sume superbiam
quaesitam meritis et mihi Delphica   15
lauro cinge volens, Melpomene, comam.

'I have completed a memorial more lasting than bronze and
higher than the royal grave of the pyramids, that neither biting rain
nor the north wind in its fury can destroy nor the unnumbered
series of years and the flight of ages (5). I shall not all die and a great
part of me shall escape the Goddess of Funerals: I shall grow ever
renewed in the praise of posterity, as long as the pontifex shall climb
the Capitol with the silent (Vestal) virgin.

'I shall be spoken of, where violent Aufidus roars (10) and where
Daunus, poor in water, has (always) ruled over his rustic peoples,
as, famous from a humble origin, having been first to spin Aeolian
poetry to Italian rhythms: take on a pride that has been won by
your merits and kindly encircle my brow, Melpomene, with
Delphic laurel.'

This is a proud and confident ode: the verb *exegi* placed at the beginning
states the poet's own achievement. But Horace is not blatant and the word
which expresses the achievement comes as a surprise: it is a tombstone—
but the word instantly evokes the usual sort of monument in the poet's
mind; a brass plaque—but his is more eternal; the 'regal mass' of the pyramids
—but his is higher. Both ideas are paradoxes: what memorial could be
more eternal (itself a paradoxical idea) than brass or higher than the pyramids.
The sentence does not pause or falter for an instant, and the mention of the
greatest of mortal memorials brings vividly to mind the forces that make all
things mortal—the biting rain, the irresistible north wind, the years without
number, the passing even of ages. It is a great sentence that starts with the
apparently tiny artefact of the poet and swells to take in the whole of human
history. The ideas are not specifically Roman: they are such as could occur
to any human being, and Pindar said something like this in *Pythian* 6. 6 ff.
where he spoke of a 'treasury of songs . . . which neither winter rains . . .
nor wind . . . can bear down to the sea . . .' But Horace's thoughts are
concentrated on his own death, and he now returns to himself to set his
own case inside a specifically Roman context. A large part of him will
escape Libitina: she was the Roman goddess of funerals and her temple in
Rome was surrounded by 'funeral parlours' and the shops of monumental
masons. There is an earthy reality about her name here that reduces the

idea of death to concrete details of the funeral and the grave. From this grim reality springs the idea (7–8) of the fresh new life which the poet, though dead, will gain from the respect of posterity, and now the poet's vision expands to take in that posterity (which will last as long as the Roman empire itself) and crystallize it in a picture of national ceremonies at the temple of Juppiter Optimus Maximus. A specifically Augustan patriotism comes to life in these lines (8–9), and this particular way of expressing it may have come to Horace from Virgil's *Aeneid* ix. 446–9; there Nisus and Euryalus have been killed and Virgil, most unusually entering the narrative in his own person, promises them immortality in his poetry 'as long as the house of Aeneas shall dwell on the eternal rock of the Capitol'. But from this great concept, which moved out from the poet's own identity (as in 3 ff.), once again the poet returns to his own individuality in a striking way: the people of the obscure little town in which he was born will speak of his poetic achievement. This touching affection for his own origins, a character-istically Italian 'campanilismo' which many Romans expressed and which can be seen to this day, is expressed in an elevated way that contrasts with the humble subject. The country is identified by its river, Aufidus, and by the legendary founder of its people (Daunus); both are epic ways of de-signating a region. The high stylistic level is marked by the imitation of a Greek construction in (12) *regnavit populorum* (where *regnare* takes a genitive, as ἄρχειν in Greek). To match this the poet describes his own poetic activity in a solemn and unusual way: he spun (*deduxisse*, with a metaphor from spinning thread and implying finely wrought work) Aeolian poetry to Italian measures. What this means is that the poet recreated Aeolian poetry in the Latin language; in doing so he transferred the rhythms of Aeolian poetry to Italy and thus created an 'Italian' sound which was quite distinct from the Aeolian sound. Here the adjective *Italos* is proleptic: that is, it describes, in advance, the result which Horace achieved, for it was only by creating such poetry that he made the rhythms Italian. To all this he adds the claim that he was first to do it. This is a claim made by most Roman poets and is probably due to a sense that, everything poetic having already been done by Greeks, a Roman could achieve originality only in respect to other Romans. Even so, he has to ignore the two Sapphic poems of Catullus (11 and 51), but this was justified because Catullus did not attempt to represent Sappho's poetry in Latin: he only made casual use of some of her themes and her metre for his own purpose.

The poem ends with an idea which could easily have seemed ridiculous: the crowning of the poet with Delphic laurel. This is a Greek idea and the laurel is Delphic because of Apollo's connection with poetry. But in a

Roman context the crowning with laurel suggests the triumphant general (and, for instance, Propertius—iii. 1. 9–12—pictures himself as such), and is close to hyperbole. But Horace has handled the idea skilfully by making the end a prayer to his Muse[1] who is asked to feel pride in achievements which are really hers, and, in token of this, to crown the poet (the tone of prayer to a deity is particularly carried by the word *volens*—cf. *laeta* 21. 21). The attitude of prayer and thanksgiving is a perfect antidote to the expression of personal pride; the pleasure he feels in the pride of his humble home-town and the prayer of thanks to the Muse are two successive steps down from the assertion of his own achievement in 1–9.

[1] Her name is not significant: see p. 50, n. 1.

APPENDIX

Some passages illustrating the Greek background to Horace, *Odes* iii

1. Alcaeus (frag. 10 Lobel and Page): see ode 12

   ἔμε δείλαν, ἔμε παίσαν κακοτάτων πεδέχοισαν
   ]δομονο[
   ]ει μόρος αἶσχ[
   ἐπὶ γὰρ πᾶρος ὀνίατον † ἰκνεῖται
   ἐλάφω δὲ βρόμος ἐν στήθεσι φυίει φοβέροισιν
   μ]αινόμενον [
   ] ἀυάται ’ ὤ [

   'Me, a woman pitiable, me, who am spared no misery... destiny of shame.
   ... For upon me comes grievous injury. The belling of the deer grows...
   in the timid heart... maddened... infatuations...' (D. L. Page's translation).

2. Pindar, *Pythian* i. 1–20: see ode 4

   Χρυσέα φόρμιγξ, Ἀπόλλωνος καὶ ἰοπλοκάμων
   σύνδικον Μοισᾶν κτέανον· τᾶς ἀκούει
      μὲν βάσις ἀγλαΐας ἀρχά,
   πείθονται δ’ ἀοιδοὶ σάμασιν
   ἀγησιχόρων ὁπόταν προοιμίων
      ἀμβολὰς τεύχῃς ἐλελιζομένα.
   καί τὸν αἰχματὰν κεραυνὸν σβεννύεις
   αἰενάου πυρός. εὕδει δ’ ἀνὰ σκά-
      πτῳ Διὸς αἰετός, ὠκεῖ-
      αν πτέρυγ’ ἀμφοτέρωθεν χαλάξαις,

   ἀρχὸς οἰωνῶν, κελαινῶπιν δ’ ἐπί οἱ νεφέλαν
   ἀγκύλῳ κρατί, γλεφάρων ἀδὺ κλάϊ-
      θρον, κατέχευας· ὁ δὲ κνώσσων

ὑγρὸν νῶτον αἰωρεῖ, τεαῖς
ῥιπαῖσι κατασχόμενος. καὶ γὰρ βια-
        τὰς Ἄρης, τραχεῖαν ἄνευθε λιπών
ἐγχέων ἀκμάν, ἰαίνει καρδίαν
κώματι, κῆλα δὲ καὶ δαιμόνων θέλ-
        γει φρένας ἀμφί τε Λατοί-
        δα σοφίᾳ βαθυκόλπων τε Μοισᾶν.

ὅσσα δὲ μὴ πεφίληκε Ζεύς, ἀτύζονται βοάν
Πιερίδων ἀίοντα, γᾶν τε καὶ πόν-
        τον κατ᾽ ἀμαιμάκετον,
ὅς τ᾽ ἐν αἰνᾷ Ταρτάρῳ κεῖται, θεῶν πολέμιος,
Τυφὼς ἑκατοντακάρανος· τόν ποτε
Κιλίκιον θρέψεν πολυώνυμον ἄντρον· νῦν γε μάν
ταί θ᾽ ὑπὲρ Κύμας ἁλιερκέες ὄχθαι
Σικελία τ᾽ αὐτοῦ πιέζει
        στέρνα λαχνάεντα· κίων δ᾽ οὐρανία συνέχει,
νιφόεσσ᾽ Αἴτνα, πάνετες χιόνος ὀξείας τιθήνα·

'Golden lyre, Apollo's possession and shared with the violet-crowned Muses, to you the dancer's step, the beginner of delight, pays heed, and poets obey your signals whenever, quivering, you create the opening of preludes that lead on the dance. You also quench the battling thunderbolt of ever-lasting fire. On the sceptre of Zeus sleeps the eagle, drooping his swift wings down on both sides, king of birds; you have poured a dark cloud over his curved head, a sweet lock upon his eyelids. As he sleeps, he ripples his supple back, overcome by waves (of melody). Even violent Ares, putting aside the harsh spear-point, joys his heart with rest, and your shafts charm the souls of the gods, through the skill of the son of Leto and the deep-bosomed Muses. But all whom Zeus does not love are terrified when they hear the voice of the Muses, over land and over the insatiable sea, and he too who dwells in grim Tartarus, an enemy of the gods, Typhos with his hundred heads who once was nurtured in the famed Cilician cave; but now the cliffs above Cyme that hold off the sea and Sicily too press hard down upon his hairy chest. And a pillar to the sky, snowy Etna, holds him, foster-nurse to chill snow all year round.'

3. Pindar, *Pythian* i. 38–40: see ode 4. 61–4.

Λύκιε καὶ Δάλοι᾽ ἀνάσσων
        Φοῖβε Παρνασσοῦ τε κράναν Κασταλίαν φιλέων,
ἐθελήσαις ταῦτα νόῳ τιθέμεν εὐανδροῦν τε χώραν.

'O Phoebus of Lycia and prince of Delos and lover of the fountain Castalia on Parnassus, be pleased to take these prayers to heart and make the land rich in fine men.'

4. Callimachus, *Hymn i (to Zeus)* 70–85: see ode 1

εἵλεο δ' αἰзηῶν ὅ τι φέρτατον· οὐ σύ γε νηῶν
ἐμπεράμους, οὐκ ἄνδρα σακέσπαλον, οὐ μὲν ἀοιδόν·
ἀλλὰ τὰ μὲν μακάρεσσιν ὀλίзοσιν αὖθι παρῆκας
ἄλλα μέλειν ἑτέροισι, σὺ δ' ἐξέλεο πτολιάρχους
αὐτούς, ὧν ὑπὸ χεῖρα γεωμόρος, ὧν ἴδρις αἰχμῆς,
ὧν ἐρέτης, ὧν πάντα· τί δ' οὐ κρατέοντος ὑπ' ἰσχύν;
αὐτίκα χαλκῆας μὲν ὑδείομεν Ἡφαίστοιο,
τευχηστὰς δ' Ἄρηος, ἐπακτῆρας δὲ Χιτώνης
Ἀρτέμιδος, Φοίβου δὲ λύρης εὖ εἰδότας οἴμους·
"ἐκ δὲ Διὸς βασιλῆες", ἐπεὶ Διὸς οὐδὲν ἀνάκτων
θειότερον· τῷ καί σφε τεὴν ἐκρίναο λάξιν.
δῶκας δὲ πτολίεθρα φυλασσέμεν, ἵзεο δ' αὐτός
ἄκρησ' ἐν πολίεσσιν, ἐπόψιος οἵ τε δίκῃσι
λαὸν ὑπὸ σκολιῇσ' οἵ τ' ἔμπαλιν ἰθύνουσιν·
ἐν δὲ ῥυηφενίην ἔβαλές σφισιν, ἐν δ' ἅλις ὄλβον·
πᾶσι μέν, οὐ μάλα δ' ἴσον.

'You chose the greatest of powerful men: neither those who are skilled in ships nor a man who wields a shield nor yet a poet; those you assigned to lesser blessed gods—to others other cares. But you chose the rulers of cities themselves, beneath whose hand is the landowner, the man skilled with the spear, the oarsman, everything—what is not under the ruler's control? Smiths, for instance, we say belong to Hephaistos, warriors to Ares, huntsmen to Artemis of the short tunic, and to Phoebus those who well know the tunes of the lyre. "From Zeus come kings", for nothing is more divine than the princes of Zeus. So you chose them for your lot and gave them cities to watch over, and yourself sat on the high places of their cities, looking out for those who rule their people with crooked judgements and for those who do the opposite. To them you gave prosperity and wealth abundantly— to all, but not equally.'

5. Agis, *Palatine Anthology* vi. 152: see ode 26

Καὶ στάλικας καὶ πτηνὰ λαγωβόλα σοί τάδε Μείδων,
Φοῖβε, σύν ἰξευταῖς ἐκρέμασεν καλάμοις,
ἔργων ἐξ ὀλίγων ὀλίγην δόσιν· ἢν δέ τι μεῖзον
δωρήσῃ, τίσει τῶνδε πολυπλάσια.

'Meidon hung up in dedication to you, Phoebus, his stakes and winged hare-killing sticks here, together with his fowling rods—a small gift from small profits. But if you should give him greater, then he will return you many times more than these.'

6. Antipater of Sidon, *Palatine Anthology* vi. 14: see ode 26

Πανὶ τάδ' αὔθαιμοι τρισσοὶ θέσαν ἄρμενα τέχνας·
Δᾶμις μὲν θηρῶν ἄρκυν ὀρειονόμων,
Κλείτωρ δὲ πλωτῶν τάδε δίκτυα, τὰν δὲ πετηνῶν
ἄρρηκτον Πίγρης τάνδε δεραιοπέδαν.
τὸν μὲν γὰρ ξυλόχων, τὸν δ' ἠέρος, ὃν δ' ἀπὸ λίμνας
οὔ ποτε σὺν κενεοῖς οἶκος ἔδεκτο λίνοις.

'Three brothers dedicated to Pan these tools of their craft; Damis his net for catching wild creatures of the mountain, Kleitor this net for fish, and Pigres this unbreakable neck-fettering net for birds. For the one from woodland, the other from the air, the third from the sea—none was ever received home with empty nets.'

7. Leonidas of Tarentum, *Palatine Anthology* vi. 13: see ode 26

Οἱ τρισσοί τοι ταῦτα τὰ δίκτυα θῆκαν ὅμαιμοι,
ἀγρότα Πάν, ἄλλης ἄλλος ἀπ' ἀγρεσίης·
ὧν ἀπὸ μὲν πτανῶν Πίγρης τάδε, ταῦτα δὲ Δᾶμις
τετραπόδων, Κλείτωρ δ' ὁ τρίτος εἰναλίων.
ἀνθ' ὧν τῷ μὲν πέμπε δι' ἠέρος εὔστοχον ἄγρην,
τῷ δὲ διὰ δρυμῶν, τῷ δὲ δι' ἠιόνων.

'The three brothers dedicated these nets to you, Pan the hunter, each from a different type of hunting: from birds Pigres this here, this Damis from animals, Kleitor the third from sea-creatures. In return for which, send the one easily caught game through the air, the other through thickets, and the third through the sea round the coasts.'

8. Leonidas of Tarentum, *Palatine Anthology* vi. 334: see odes 13 and 22

Αὔλια καὶ Νυμφέων ἱερὸς πάγος αἵ θ' ὑπὸ πέτρῃ
πίδακες ἥ θ' ὕδασιν γειτονέουσα πίτυς
καὶ σὺ τετραγλώχιν, μηλοσσόε, Μαιάδος Ἑρμᾶ,
ὅς τε τὸν αἰγιβότην, Πάν, κατέχεις σκόπελον,
ἵλαοι τὰ ψαιστὰ τό τε σκύφος, ἔμπλεον οἴνης
δέξασθ', Αἰακίδεω δῶρα Νεοπτολέμου.

'Caves and sacred hill of the Nymphs, and springs beneath the rock, and the pine that stands neighbour to the waters, and you, rectangular Hermes, son of Maia, guardian of sheep, and you, Pan, who control the rock where goats feed, kindly accept these cakes and cup filled with wine, the gifts of Neoptolemus, descendant of Aeacus.'

9. Leonidas of Tarentum, *Palatine Anthology* ix. 326: see ode 13

Πέτρης ἐκ δισσῆς ψυχρὸν κατεπάλμενον ὕδωρ,
χαίροις, καὶ Νυμφέων ποιμενικὰ ξόανα
πέτραι τε κρηνέων καὶ ἐν ὕδασι κόσμια ταῦτα
ὑμέων, ὦ κοῦραι, μυρία τεγγόμενα,
χαίρετ᾽· Ἀριστοκλέης ὅδ᾽ ὁδοιπόρος, ᾧπερ ἀπῶσα
δίψαν βαψάμενος, τοῦτο δίδωμι γέρας.

'Hail, cold stream leaping down from the cleft rock and images of nymphs dedicated by shepherds, and rocks of the springs and these thousands of figurines of you, Nymphs, drenched with the waters, hail. I Aristokles, a wayfarer, present to you this cup which I dipped in your stream to quench my thirst.'

10. Philodemus, *Palatine Anthology* xi. 44: see odes 8, 14 (17–28), 17, 19, 21, 28, and 29

Αὔριον εἰς λιτήν σε καλιάδα, φίλτατε Πείσων,
ἐξ ἐνάτης ἕλκει μουσοφιλὴς ἕταρος
εἰκάδα δειπνίζων ἐνιαύσιον· εἰ δ᾽ ἀπολείψεις
οὔθατα καὶ Βρομίου Χιογενῆ πρόποσιν,
ἀλλ᾽ ἑτάρους ὄψει παναληθέας, ἀλλ᾽ ἐπακούσῃ
Φαιήκων γαίης πουλὺ μελιχρότερα·
ἢν δέ ποτε στρέψῃς καὶ ἐς ἡμέας ὄμματα, Πείσων,
ἄξομεν ἐκ λιτῆς εἰκάδα πιοτέρην.

'Tomorrow, dearest Piso, your friend who is loved by the Muses invites you to his humble cottage after the ninth hour as he keeps the annual feast of the twentieth [the birthday of Epicurus]. And if you will miss cooked udders and draughts of Chian-born wine, at least you will meet the truest of friends, at least you will listen to words far sweeter than in the land of the Phaeacians. But if ever you should turn your eyes to me also, Piso, then, instead of a humble twentieth, we shall celebrate a far richer one.'

11. Moschus, *Europe* 115–28 and 153–66: see ode 27.

ἡ δὲ τότ᾿ ἐρχομένοιο γαληνιάασκε θάλασσα,   115
κήτεα δ᾿ ἀμφὶς ἄταλλε Διὸς προπάροιθε ποδοῖιν,
γηθόσυνος δ᾿ ὑπὲρ οἶδμα κυβίστεε βυσσόθε δελφίς.
Νηρεΐδες δ᾿ ἀνέδυσαν ὑπὲξ ἁλός, αἱ δ᾿ ἄρα πᾶσαι
κητείοις νώτοισιν ἐφήμεναι ἐστιχόωντο.
καὶ δ᾿ αὐτὸς βαρύδουπος ὑπεὶρ ἅλα ᾿Εννοσίγαιος   120
κῦμα κατιθύνων ἁλίης ἡγεῖτο κελεύθου
αὐτοκασιγνήτῳ· τοὶ δ᾿ ἀμφί μιν ἠγερέθοντο
Τρίτωνες, πόντοιο βαρύθροοι αὐλητῆρες,
κόχλοισιν ταναοῖς γάμιον μέλος ἠπύοντες.
ἡ δ᾿ ἄρ᾿ ἐφεζομένη Ζηνὸς βοέοις ἐπὶ νώτοις   125
τῇ μὲν ἔχεν ταύρου δολιχὸν κέρας, ἐν χερὶ δ᾿ ἄλλῃ
εἴρυε πορφυρέην κόλπου πτύχα ὄφρά κε μή μιν
δεύοι ἐφελκόμενον πολιῆς ἁλὸς ἄσπετον ὕδωρ.

                          .   .   .   .

  ῝Ως φάτο· τὴν δ᾿ ὧδε προσεφώνεεν ἠύκερως βοῦς·
"θάρσει παρθενική· μὴ δείδιθι πόντιον οἶδμα.
αὐτός τοι Ζεύς εἰμι, κεὶ ἐγγύθεν εἴδομαι εἶναι   155
ταῦρος, ἐπεὶ δύναμαί γε φανήμεναι ὅττι θέλοιμι.
σὸς δὲ πόθος μ᾿ ἀνέηκε τόσην ἅλα μετρήσασθαι
ταύρῳ ἐειδόμενον. Κρήτη δέ σε δέξεται ἤδη
ἥ μ᾿ ἔθρεψε καὶ αὐτόν, ὅπῃ νυμφήια σεῖο
ἔσσεται· ἐξ ἐμέθεν δὲ κλυτοὺς φιτύσεαι υἷας   160
οἳ σκηπτοῦχοι ἅπαντες ἐπιχθονίοισιν ἔσονται."
  ῝Ως φάτο· καὶ τετέλεστο τά περ φάτο. φαίνετο μὲν δή
Κρήτη, Ζεὺς δὲ πάλιν σφετέρην ἀνελάζετο μορφήν
λῦσε δέ οἱ μίτρην, καί οἱ λέχος ἔντυον ῟Ωραι.
ἡ δὲ πάρος κούρη Ζηνὸς γένετ᾿ αὐτίκα νύμφη,   165
καὶ Κρονίδῃ τέκε τέκνα καὶ αὐτίκα γίνετο μήτηρ.

'And the sea, as he came to it, grew calm, and the monsters gambolled around before the feet of Zeus and dolphins joyfully tumbled over the waves from the depths of the sea; and Nereids rose from the sea and all of them, riding on the backs of monsters, came row upon row. The deep-rumbling Earth-Shaker himself (120) led the way over the sea, controlling the waves of the briny pathway for his brother. Around him the Tritons gathered, the deep-sounding flautists of the sea, playing a marriage-tune on their long slim shells. But she sitting upon the bull's back of Zeus (125), with one hand held the bull's long horn, and with the other caught up the crimson fold of her robe so that it should not become wet dragged through the endless waters of the grey sea. . . . So she spoke, and thus the horned bull addressed her: "Courage, maiden: do not fear the sea-wave. I am Zeus himself—even if from nearby I seem to be a bull (155)—for I can appear whatever I wish. Desire for you caused me to measure out so long a sea-journey in the likeness of a bull. Crete, which nursed me, will soon receive you and there shall your wedding be. From me you shall conceive famed sons (160), all of whom shall be kings to men on earth." So he spoke and it happened as he said. Crete came in sight, Zeus took on again his own form and he unloosed her girdle and the Horai made her bed for her. She who was a virgin then became the bride of Zeus; and to the son of Kronos she bore children, becoming a mother.'

INDEX

Acastus, 69.
Acrisius, 100.
Actium, battle of, 4, 63, 128.
adscribere ('enrol'), 43.
Adultery, 5, 64, 65, 77–9, 126 ff.
Aegyptus, 83.
Aelius Lamia, L. (*cos.* A.D. 3), 104–5.
'Aeolian' poetry, 151.
Africa, a Roman province, 102 n. 1.
Agis, 156.
Alcaeus, 11, 86, 151, 153.
Alcaic line, initial short syllable in, 60 n. 2.
Alien political systems, 30, 100, 116–17.
Amoebean song, 75–6.
Amphiaraus, 100.
Amphion, 82.
Anaphora, 82, 89, 116.
Antiochus, 64.
Antipater of Sidon, 156.
arbiter bibendi, 72–4, 110–11.
Archaisms, 12, 69.
Artemis Eileithyia, 118.
Asyndeton, 15–16, 53, 72, 107.
Atilius Regulus, M., 58 ff.
atqui, 60, 69.
attonitus ('inspired'), 111.
Aufidus, 151.
Augur, 110.
aulaea, 147.
αὐτάρκεια, 32, 148.
authepsa, 110 n. 1.
Autobiographical details, poetic use of, 51, 53–4, 82–3, 140–1.

Bacchus, 42, 72, 129–31.
Bacchus and poetic inspiration, 111, 129–31.
Bactria, 147.
Baiae, 51.
Bellerophon, 69.
Bithynia, 69–70.
Blending of Greek and Roman, 20, 30, 31, 69–70, 78–9, 87, 97, 106–8, 110–12, 118.

Blood-sacrifice, 88–90, 118.
bonus dies as ritual term, 116.
Britain, 51, 57, 59.

Callimachus 31, 88 n. 1, 95, 154–5.
Calliope, 50.
Calpurnius Bibulus, M. (*cos.* 59 B.C.), 143.
'Campanilismo', 151.
Capitol as symbol of empire, 43, 58, 151.
carpe diem, difficult advice to give Maecenas, 73–4, 148.
Cato, M. (censor 184 B.C.), 116, 121.
Catullus, 8–9, 10, 11–12, 64 n. 1, 67, 75, 95, 151.
Cerberus, 82, 84–5.
cessans, 143.
cetera in sense of 'the future', 148.
Choral and monodic lyric, difference between, 50 n. 2, 53–54.
Civil war, fear of, 4 f., 65–6, 127–8.
Claudian, 67.
Codrus, 109.
collegia iuuenum, 35 n. 2.
Communism, primitive, 14 f., 126–8.
condicio in poetry, 18, 58.
Country life, ideal of, 30, 32, 64, 102, 103.
Cranes, ancient, 78.
Croesus, 75, 102.
Cyprus, 133.

Dacia, 63, 73.
Danaë, 100.
Danaus, daughters of, 82–3.
Danger in poetic inspiration, 131.
Daunus, 151.
de, meanings of, 67.
de tenero ungui, 63, 66–7.
Decidius Saxa, L. (*tr. pl.* 44 B.C.), 63.
Dedicatory epigrams, 89, 133.
deducere (spinning metaphor), 151.
Deification (of Augustus) by association, 42, 57 n. 2, 59, 92.

PRINTED IN GREAT BRITAIN
AT THE UNIVERSITY PRESS, OXFORD
BY VIVIAN RIDLER
PRINTER TO THE UNIVERSITY